BLACK BRANT

SEA GOOSE OF THE PACIFIC COAST

BLACK BRANT

SEA GOOSE OF THE PACIFIC COAST

ARTHUR S. EINARSEN

Published by agreement with the
United States Department of the Interior,
Fish and Wildlife Service,
Bureau of Sport Fisheries and Wildlife

UNIVERSITY OF WASHINGTON PRESS   Seattle   1965

Library of Congress Catalog Card Number 63-10796
Manufactured by George Banta Company, Inc., Menasha, Wisconsin
Printed in the United States of America

Foreword

The environment of the black brant is the rugged coast of the Pacific Northwest, where this elusive, wild sea goose makes its first landfall on its autumn migration across a corner of the Pacific from the Alaskan Peninsula. This was the scene of the author's early acquaintance with the black brant, which symbolized his home country and all the experiences of childhood.

Whenever and wherever one encounters it in later years, a particular species of wildlife evokes nostalgic recollections of youthful enthusiasms. All too frequently this is a pathway to disappointment because the familiar scenes of youth have been completely changed by developments we associate with progress. Need there be a better reason for preserving some of the natural environments with which our nation was once so bountifully endowed? In my judgment Americans of the future should be able not only to bring to mind the joys of contact with nature in their impressionable youth, but also be able to go back occasionally during a busy, sometimes frustrating life, and re-experience these pleasures. Nowhere else can the same personal satisfaction be found than in those places which combine the thrilling sights, sounds and smells of early youth. Here one can gain new energy and fresh perspective unfound in pill, palliative, or artifact.

In this volume, Arthur S. Einarsen illustrates very well the need for preserving the naturalness of the rapidly changing Pacific coastline, its strands, promontories, and protected bays. Undefiled habitat is necessary so that the black brant, important alike to Eskimo, Aleut, and wildfowler, can find haven and food. It is also essential if the boys and girls and the men and women of tomorrow are to enjoy our wildlife in its incomparable natural setting.

STEWART L. UDALL
Secretary of the Interior

Preface

In everyone's mind there are recollections so vivid that he can easily relive past experiences. How clearly I remember a day in late November, 1903, when the smell of burning peat moss was in the air. I was a little boy standing on the barrier beach of Livingston Bay and looking out across the water to Mt. Rainier. The incoming tide lapped softly against the massive driftwood piled high on the beach, and the glassy surface of the bay was broken only where widgeons cruised leisurely, cutting V-shaped ripples as they searched for food. Cattle were lowing in the nearby meadows; cowbells tinkled as the dairy herd moved toward the barn, urged by the shepherd dog; and from the sea came a compelling and eerie call, vibrant and reedlike.

Thoughtfully I wandered back to my home at the edge of the meadow, and in the glow of the kitchen lamp I tried to tell my parents about the mysterious music I had heard over the water. "It must have been some bird," said my mother. To this day these haunting notes stir within me mental pictures of the sunset, the sea, the burnished water of the bay, and the silhouette of flying birds against a deep rosy sky.

For several years thereafter I was charmed and awed by the music that periodically came across the open water, but I had only a distant glimpse of some birds that might, perhaps, be responsible for those ringing notes, which ended almost as soon as they began. It was some time later, on this same Washington bay, that I came upon a living, resting group on the sand bar at the Big Spit and was able to lie in the driftwood and watch them preen, wax their feathers, and rest at their chosen haven. I learned that this was the Pacific black brant, *Branta bernicla nigricans,* and its fascination has lived with me these many years without diminishing.

Since the Pacific black brant is generally unknown, except to a few ornithologists and dedicated brant hunters, its life story and migration have been only sketchily recorded. The conservationist has no clear-cut guide in dealing with the species. This is reflected in the varied management regulations throughout its range. In many ways its survival is in jeopardy. The species has been long native to the west coast of North America. The American Ornithologists Union *Check-list of North American Birds* (1931) records its presence during the Pleistocene period in Fossil Lake in Oregon. Mute evidence of its presence is found in the earthy deposits of a prehistoric seaside edge now far inland, while today it frequents the sea edge from the Arctic to Baja California.

The little that has been written about black brant is found more often in the terse notes of explorers or naturalists who sought out the sea edge. In this material there are few contributions to the life story of the bird, although sight records and distribution were recorded. A general knowledge of habitat occupancy during the last half of the past century can be drawn. These early records, developed by limited personnel, assessing the potential of a new land, found little encouragement or demand for a detailed study of individual species. This came later, as the West Coast population developed a few naturalist and conservation workers through both interest and assignment as a part of their responsibility. James Moffitt, as an interested young naturalist and hunter and then as the economic biologist of the State of California Game Department, made the first studies of brant population and initiated the first census of the species. His state-wide surveys grew into regional activities. His last work, in the early forties, came at the beginning of a new era when improved airplanes were being used for census work. At the end of the second world war, equipment became available to bring people to the remote areas sought out by the nesting black brant. Inventory methods became a regular part of management.

Personnel of the U.S. Fish and Wildlife Service, particularly Charles E. Gillham, whose travel by outboard motor and small boats along the Arctic rim, and Robert Smith, who for many years has flown the Pacific and Arctic coasts, together with the cooperation of Canadian workers, compiled a better knowledge of the habitat of the black brant. Their work to a large degree defined the limits of the brant's important habitat and nesting areas. This was supplemented later by the workers of the U.S. Fish and Wildlife Service in Alaska, particularly Urban Nelson and Henry A. Hansen, who were the first to begin a real search into the life of the black brant by their nesting and banding studies on the vast flats of the Yukon and Kuskokwim rivers. Their observations and banding programs made available many facets of the brant's life story. There has been a gradual increase in the interest in the life story of this bird which has been particularly influenced by the workers in the Pacific Coast states of California, Oregon, and Washington, and the province of British Columbia. For the past fourteen years, Flyway representatives in Region 1 of the U.S. Bureau of Sport Fisheries and Wildlife at Portland, Oregon, have systematically compiled and released the survey data of the species.

This monograph is written as an attempt to engender a better common understanding of the brant's living habits, the hazards to its survival, and the means by which better management of the species can be obtained so that this fine bird of limited numbers which is a part of our heritage can be with us for many years. To follow the brant through its life cycle and its orbit seems an objective approach to attain this end.

Acknowledgments

This attempt to tell the story of the black brant rests on the interest and generosity of several organizations. The Arctic Institute graciously supported our first steps; the National Wildlife Federation offered financial support and encouragement; the Wildlife Management Institute, which for the past two decades has been outstanding in its offers of spontaneous help and heartening encouragement to worthy movements to sustain wildlife, again volunteered its aid and its solid support; the U.S. Fish and Wildlife Service, in which I was employed, carried a part of the financial burden and extended other useful aid, particularly through its field personnel. These men helped in planning field trips so that entrance into remote areas was possible, and by their self-effacing and generous efforts they facilitated preparation of the manuscript by providing factual data spanning many years.

I am grateful, too, for the generous support of the game management agencies of Oregon, Washington, and California. Friendly liaison was maintained also with the Mexican authorities and with various government and private observers in British Columbia.

If I were to single out one person from whom I received the greatest stimulation in attempting to follow the orbit of the black brant, it would be the late James (Jim) Moffitt, whose dramatic and productive career was ended in the early World War II days in a plane crash in Alaska. From early boyhood he saw more in the outdoors than the average person sees. As a naturalist he had the keenest powers of observation. When Jim learned that the black brant had become a special interest of mine, he encouraged me in following the species. It is a fond hope that some day both the hunter and the naturalist will join in dedicating a sanctuary for the black brant, preferably on Humboldt, Tomales, or Morro bays in California, and name it the "James Moffitt Wildlife Refuge."

The field notes and personal advice of C. E. Gillham, formerly of the U.S. Fish and Wildlife Service and recently retired, bring a broad scope of knowledge to the changing conditions that face the black brant. Other helpful aid was received from Henry A. Hansen and Urban C. Nelson of the U.S. Fish and Wildlife Service, Juneau, Alaska. Their organization of field work has resulted in a greater knowledge of the black brant in Alaska. Their brant banding work on the Yukon–Kuskokwim delta, accomplished despite great odds, produced a wealth of material on the life story of the brant on that part of their range. Their knowledge of the habitat and problems of the black brant released in several publications has brought into focus the plight of the species.

The detailed help of John E. Chattin, the Pacific Flyway representative of the Regional Office of the U.S. Fish and Wildlife Service in Portland, Oregon, is greatly appreciated. He searched records and compiled material that lessened fieldwork needed for the preparation of this manuscript.

The personal and cheerful help of John Adair on the nesting grounds of the Yukon–Kuskokwim delta and his contribution of camera studies are acknowledged with deep appreciation.

Robert Jones and Sam Harbow offered guidance and an intimate knowledge of the habits of brant in the Bristol Bay area, and particularly in the vital Izembek Bay.

In British Columbia, fine support was received from individuals with a particular interest in the black brant. The field notes of Theed Pearse, a pioneer and persistent recorder of brant data, add measurably to knowledge of the birds' habits in this range. That his conclusions and data are well founded rests in the fact that, after many years of devoted interest, and although now in his eighties, he still treads the beach line. Well-used trails stretching for miles up the coast are tangible evidence of his devotion, earnestness, and thoroughness, which his field notes attest.

My thanks also go to Jack Beban of Nanaimo, B.C. He and his pilot, Ken Wright, graciously offered a personally conducted aerial tour of the late wintering grounds of the black brant on the easterly shores of Vancouver Island; also extremely helpful was Beban's detailed knowledge of the habits and hunting of the bird on both sides of Vancouver Island.

I am happy to acknowledge the help of William Q. Wick. Keen interest in our wild things and the willingness to devote time to their welfare made L. F. Schneider a close companion on many memorable ventures and a source of encouragement. Study slides from Don Mitchell, formerly a game commissioner in Oregon, were very helpful. I wish especially to acknowledge the fine cooperation of Wesley Batterson of the Oregon State Game Commission, who from boyhood has been one of the outstanding observers of wildlife in his home area. Many of his contributions show an insight into the life of the brant that could not have come without his enthusiasm, patience, and devotion.

I also extend grateful appreciation to R. E. Dimick, who for the last twenty-four years has been a continual source of information and an enthusiastic companion in any venture; and to independent workers such as Stuart L. Murrell of Arcata, California, Tom Tollman of Morro Bay, Laidlaw Williams of Monterey, and the late James Monro, each of whom shared detailed experiences and data on some segment of the brant's orbit.

ARTHUR S. EINARSEN

Contents

Illustrations

TABLES

BLACK BRANT

SEA GOOSE OF THE PACIFIC COAST

1

The Black Brant: Classification and Description

The life story of the Pacific black brant begins on the tundras of the North. For the Eskimo, the first flight of the black brant marks the opening of the hunting season, the end of the long winter. After the months spent in visiting between villages; in games of skill and recreation; carving; and making and repairing paddles, spears, dog whips, and other equipment, it is time to replenish the larder with fresh meat.

For several weeks the birds fly by in wavering lines, moving with rapid wingbeats toward their traditional havens, where they rest, choose their nesting sites, lay their eggs, incubate and rear their broods. Then, after a long period of physical preparation for the flight, most brant swing southward in late fall, cross the North Pacific Ocean, and eventually make a landfall in warmer climates. During this flight they are rarely seen by man except when they leave their feeding areas in the North and when they near land again as a wavy line on the seaward horizon. They may be spotted skimming over the ocean's inner reaches to pass through a harbor entrance, or over a low headland or sandspit in straggling flocks, entering the coastal bays and lagoons for perhaps a winter stay in Washington, Oregon, or California, with Baja California their favored rendezvous. From the southern reaches of their orbit there is a gradual mid-winter swing back as they retrace their flight to enter the bays on the California, Oregon, and Washington coasts, and finally in early spring reach into British Columbia for a short distance. Then they are off again to the tundras of Alaska, and another cycle is complete.

CLASSIFICATION

The black brant is known commonly in different geographical areas by such names as brant, brent, brent goose, Eskimo goose, Pacific black brant, Pacific sea brant, and China goose. Among the Eskimos, who live more closely with the brant then any other people, the local names, in the manner of a native people, are an attempt to duplicate the voice sounds or calls of the species. Examples are: *nig lik' nuk, nuk la nuk,* and similar imitations of the brant's calls.

Accepting the taxonomy and distribution as given in the fifth edition (1957) of the A.O.U. *Check-list of North American Birds,* this book deals particularly with *Branta bernicla nigricans,* described originally by George N. Lawrence in 1846 from a specimen taken at Egg Harbor, New Jersey, which was no doubt a straggler from its usual migratory orbit. In *Arctic Birds of Canada* (1957), Snyder comments on certain unresolved problems of classification of the brant, but in the end resorts also to the long-used taxonomic terminology of the A.O.U.

There are records of the black brant's appearance in such widely separated places as Maui Island in the Hawaiian group and Cobb's Island in Virginia. A similar occurrence of widespread distribution can be noted in the drift of the Atlantic brant, *Branta bernicla hrota* (see Fig. 1). These birds, common to the eastern coast of North America, have been observed as small flocks or stragglers in the Pacific Northwest or found in a day's hunting bag. H. M. Laing found a report in a 1903 diary of Major Allan Brooks that the Atlantic brant was quite common in British Columbia; Brooks had shot eight, and in company with the late James Moffitt, he saw them on Tomales Bay, California, while they were making a brant census. Laing also reported that in May, 1934, J. B. Semple and Dr. George M. Sutton took several Atlantic brant from a flock near Campbell River, B.C.

DESCRIPTION

Since both black brant, *Brant bernicla nigricans,* and Atlantic brant, *Branta bernicla hrota,* may intermingle at the nesting grounds or in the bags of hunters along the Atlantic and Pacific coasts, some differences in their characteristics should be noted. The Pacific black brant, common on the Pacific coastal waters as far south as Magdalena Bay on the lower California peninsula, and occasionally even further southward in winter has a lead-black breast, neck, and head, a small shiny black bill, and a throat collar of white, approximately an inch in width and encircling both sides of the neck without closing in back (see Fig. 2). The gap, which is a basic leaden black color on the back of the neck, varies in width from one-half to one inch. Coloration of the breast, neck, and head of the Atlantic brant is a much lighter shade of black. Instead of having an encircling "chokerlike" band of white around the neck similar to the pattern on the Pacific brant, it has decorative white markings on the sides of the neck in about the same position, but the band has a gap both on the throat and in back. There is no solid white in the band on either species to make up this characteristic neck marking. A bird in the hand shows a scattering of white feathers which on close inspection looks mottled, while a bird at a distance on the water will appear to have a solid band, choker, or collar of white.

The black brant underbody has no fine-line color differentiation at the turn of the breast. Rather, it shades off into a lighter and lighter shade of slate or gray, finally blending into snowy white on the posterior approximately five inches from the tail. Upon close scrutiny, the Atlantic brant has a very sharp line of color differentiation at the turn of the breast and the underbody, a light gray blending into the snowy-white posterior portion of the bird about seven inches from the tail. A comparison of study skins shows that the white portion of the posterior underbody of the black brant usually begins opposite the knee joint in the crossed legs of museum specimens. On the Atlantic brant, the white color pattern extends almost two inches in front of this definite location. When birds of these two groups are laid side by side, the difference in color is obvious although size and weight may be identical. It would be almost impossible, then, to separate the Atlantic from the Pacific brant when they are in the air.

This small marine goose of the Pacific coastal habitats has an average weight of about three pounds, though it may vary from between two and one-half to three and one-half pounds. Table 1 shows typical weights of brant in comparison with cackling and white-fronted geese. When the young of the year are at hand, the factor of weight cannot be considered as indicative of age class or maturity. Food is ample on the nesting grounds, the days are long, these young grow very rapidly, and by the time of fall migration may weigh nearly as much as the adults. The difference becomes marked when the adults have recovered from their long summer vigil in the care of their brood. Coloration is a better indicator of age class. The scapulars, wing coverts, and

TABLE I

WEIGHTS OF GEESE, JULY 1949 AND 1950, ON THE YUKON–
KUSKOKWIM DELTA, ALASKA*

SPECIES	SAM-PLE	AGE CLASS	SEX	WEIGHT (IN OUNCES)		
				Mini-mum	Maxi-mum	Aver-age
Black brant	17	Adult over one year	F	37	54	46
Black brant	5	Adult first year	F	39	47	43
Black brant	11	Adult over one year	M	41	60	52
Black brant	5	Adult first year	M	38	54	47
Black brant	33	Adults (all age classes)	F	35	54	44
Black brant	22	Adults (all age classes)	M	38	60	49
Black brant	55	Adults (all age classes)	M&F	35	60	46
Cackling geese	?	Adults (all age classes)	F	45	59	51
Cackling geese	11	Adults (all age classes)	M	49	64	56
White-fronted geese	1	Adults (all age classes)	F	—	—	96

* U.S. Fish and Wildlife Service, Alaska Staff.

secondaries in the young of the year show a tipping or edging with an offshade of white. In the adults, the same area is a solid lead-black color. On the juvenile black brant, the neck band or collar is even more mottled than on the adult, and when the bird of the year is taken in the hunting harvest this neck pattern means it is immature (see Fig. 3).

Brant resting on the water seem to have a short neck, but this is not true when they are feeding. In this situation the brant stretches its neck to gain elevation, thus increasing its scanning powers. This imparts a grotesque disproportion, since its head and bill are quite small, and the bird loses its symmetrical appearance. In flight the neck does not seem to compare with that of any other *Branta*. The western Canadas in particular, when coursing slowly over the marshlands, meadows, or grainfields, expose an unusually long neck, exceeded only by that of the swan.

When flying, the brant seems compact and closely coupled, its body quite ducklike. It appears shorter in body length than it really is, because of the white color on both the back and rump portions. When viewed against the sea or cloud formations, its silhouette seems to end with dark feathers on the wing and back areas—a further aid to the hunter or bird watcher in properly differentiating brant from other geese at a distance.

In manners, voice, pitch, calls, and habits, the black brant has very little similarity with the other *Branta* groups known generally as Canada geese. Its silhouette, or outline against a glassy sea, is much closer to that of the barnacle goose, *Branta leucopsis*, of Europe than to the above-mentioned *Branta* on the North American continent. If the white cheek patch of the barnacle goose were painted out on a photograph, the two birds look alike. Certainly its marine habits set the brant apart from the wide-ranging land forms with which it is classed taxonomically.

The description of the black brant commonly used in current bird books combines the observations of several workers, although the voluminous and authoritative publications of Arthur Cleveland Bent are greatly in evidence in most treatises. A composite of these descriptions will be used and properly identified to offer a description of the adults, the very young (see Fig. 4), and the juveniles:

ADULTS, BOTH SEXES. Head and neck, leaden black, except for white collar at top of neck, incomplete behind; bill, black; eye, dark brown. Body, chest, and foreback, leaden black (sometimes blending into slaty breast); back and scapulars, brownish black, feathers slightly paler at tips; rump, brownish black, with sides of rump, white; breast, brown, barred with white or whitish; belly and flanks, whitish; feet, black. Tail, black; upper and under coverts, white, usually as long as, and sometimes slightly longer than, tail. Wings, all coverts, like back; all flight feathers, dull black; lining and axillars, greyish brown. (Kortright, 1942) *Size:* Length 22-29, wing 12.70-13.50, bill 1.20-1.35. (Bailey, 1902)

DOWNY YOUNG. The downy young black brant is thickly covered with soft down in dark colors; the upper half of the head, including the lores, to a point a little below the eyes is "fuscous" or "benzo brown"; the chin is white; the back varies from "benzo brown" to "hair brown," darkest on the rump; the flanks and chest shade from "hair brown" to "light drab," fading off nearly to white on the belly and throat. (Bent, 1925) *Young:* White collar indistinct or wanting; larger wing coverts and secondaries broadly tipped with white. (Bailey, 1902)

JUVENILE. During first autumn, similar in general coloration to adult but more greyish; scapulars, secondaries and wing coverts, brown, tipped with white, with considerable variation in broadness of white tipping in coverts; white collar of adult not evident and no barring on sides; breast, dark grey to blackish. After complete moult during summer, plumage fully adult. (Kortright, 1942)

2

Distribution

It is one hundred and nineteen years since George N. Lawrence first described the black brant. We are still not fully aware of all the havens in their annual orbit. Complete knowledge of their far-reaching habitat will soon be attained. Isolation, particularly on the fringes of the Arctic, will not prevent us from recording their extensive journey for now the sea, sky, ice, and land can be scanned by the increasing use of airplanes and helicopters.

SEASONAL RANGE

Until we have a full picture of their orbit, it seems wise to describe the known limits, using the outline of distribution found in the A.O.U. *Check-list* and more recent observations.

Branta nigricans, Black brant, Lawrence (1846).

Breeds in the arctic maritime regions of eastern Asia and western North America, from the Taimyr Peninsula, the Yenisei River, and the New Siberian Islands east to northern Alaska and northwestern Canada (Coronation Gulf, the arctic islands around Banks Island, Prince Patrick Island, and Melville Island, east to about long. 110° W.); south to Nelson Island, Alaska, and northeastern Mackenzie.

Winters chiefly on the Pacific coast of North America, from the Queen Charlotte Islands and Vancouver Island, British Columbia, south to Baja California (where it is common south to Magdalena Bay), inland to Malheur and Klamath lakes, Oregon, Tule Lake, California, and Pyramid and Washoe lakes, Nevada; also to Bering Island, Kamchatka, the Kuriles, Korea, Japan, and northern China (Tsingtao).

Casual in Wyoming, Utah, and Texas; accidental in the Hawaiian Islands

(Maui), Massachusetts (near Chatham), New York (Long Island), New Jersey (Egg Harbor), and Virginia (Cobb's Island).

A detailed search for records of observations of the black brant will reveal the basic pattern outlined in the A.O.U. *Check-list* and the periodic occupancy of habitat is covered by the above terse description. Partial verification is found in the book of E. A. Preble and C. Hart Merriam (1908) in their search for data on the black brant. They offer the following information on their presence in the Canadian and Alaska Arctic:

The black brant inhabits the Arctic coast east at least to Franklin Bay, and northeastwardly on the islands. Judging by what has been recorded concerning their migration route, it is reasonably certain that the brent geese which visit Banks Land and Melville Islands are of this species. Though keeping strictly to the seacoast east of the Mackenzie during migration, many of the flocks (probably all the eastern breeding birds) strike across Alaska from near the mouth of the Mackenzie to the north Pacific.

Very little is known regarding the boundaries of the breeding ranges of this and the preceding species, but it is probable that the following records refer to *B. nigricans.*

Sabine states that brent geese breed in great numbers on the islands of the Polar Sea, referring particularly to Melville Island, since Fisher in his account of the same expedition states that many were seen near Liddon Gulf (and elsewhere) in June, 1820.

Armstrong records large numbers of brent geese seen on Banks Land, near Prince Alfred Cape, August 19, 1851.

Baird, Brewer, and Ridgway state that Mr. MacFarlane found it breeding in abundance on islands northeast of the mouth of Anderson River, in Liverpool Bay, on the Arctic coast, on Franklin Bay, on various other parts of the coast, and especially in regions west of Anderson River.

Salvadori records a skin from Liverpool Bay, collected by MacFarlane.

Reed records eggs from Cape Bathurst, taken June 22, 1901, by H. H. Bodfish.

Richardson observed "brent geese," undoubtedly of this species; near Cape Bathurst on August 11, 1848, and refers to the circumstances as follows: The eider ducks had now assembled in immense flocks and with the brent geese were migrating to the westward. Both these waterfowl follow the coast line in their migrations. . . . The brents are not seen inland to the eastward of Peel's River.

In the same work Richardson published extracts from a letter from Mr. Murray, describing a black goose which regularly passed through the Yukon Valley in migration, the description plainly referring to this species. A few of the birds were said to pass down Peel River, "but they are more abundant on the Yukon."

As confirming evidence that the bird uses a portion of the valley of the Yukon as a migration route, the following paragraph by Baird, Brewer, and Ridgway (1884) is of interest.

Mr. Kennicott, in a note dated Fort Yukon, May 19, refers to procuring these specimens of this bird known in that region as the "Eskimo Geese." He states that it arrives there the latest of all the birds, and after nearly all the other Geese have passed. It flies in large flocks and very rapidly. The three specimens were the first noticed that season, and the only ones killed, although two dozen or more flocks of from 25 to 50 were seen in all, but in no comparison, in point of numbers, with the other four species. This bird is said to pass La Pierre House in immense numbers both in spring and fall.

Cade in a recent work (1953) confirms flights to the Arctic by way of the Yukon River, but obviously the birds are much fewer in number than in the days referred to by the foregoing authors. Most workers familiar with brant migrations report the southward drift in the fall along the Arctic coast and not through the inland passes.

More recent observations on brant in the subarctic are found in Herbert Brandt's *Alaska Bird Trails* (1943) and *The Birds of Alaska* (1959) by Ira N. Gabrielson and Frederick C. Lincoln. Brandt spent a spring season on Hooper Bay in 1924 and noted the migratory flights passing that point in mid-May. He stated that "the black brant was very numerous as a bird of passage, passing over Point Dall by thousands, but from all the information we could gather it has never bred in the vicinity." His experience in accepting the impression that brant did not nest in the locality where he made his observations concurs with reports from many areas. Brant are extremely selective in their nesting areas, but are also so gregarious that, unless keen attention or chance reveals their concentration, a nesting colony may be completely overlooked in the vast stretch of available nesting habitat. (See Fig. 5.) For many years workers by-passed well-favored sea edges, such as Hooper Bay, deceived into missing the nesting range by only a few miles. Since there is little evidence of birds in extensive flights at nesting time unless they are disturbed, a colony may be near at hand and still remain unnoticed.

Gabrielson (1959) studied the brant in Alaska in July, 1946, and again in late June and early July, 1951. He records nesting brant in Hazen Bay and Shishmaref areas, but not in the numbers recorded from the more favored tidal edges in the Yukon–Kuskokwim delta areas by field workers of the U.S. Fish and Wildlife Service and the Alaska Game Commission staff.

Unfortunately, no statistical data were provided by the early explorers such as Sabine, who noted brant near Liddon Gulf in June, 1880, or Armstrong, who mentions "large numbers of brent geese seen on

Banksland near Prince Alfred Cape on August 19, 1851." It must be presumed that "large numbers" signifies relative abundance. There were obviously enough brant to be noticeable, and perhaps they were regarded as a source of food, though in this situation they may still have been a small segment of the total breeding population in the northland. In recent years the work of Gillham and Smith, Flyway biologists of the U.S. Fish and Wildlife Service, along the North American Arctic rim seems to indicate a substantial reduction in the numbers present on the east end of the brant's migratory orbit, for both observers have commented on their general scarcity there in comparison with the areas now known to hold the greater segments of the Pacific sea brant population.

Marine areas between the Arctic nesting ground and the most southerly wintering areas show a different use pattern from that of earlier reports. (See Chart 1.) There are records of small numbers of birds that winter in a few isolated sections along the Aleutian chain and at the Sanak reefs and are scattered in a similar way along some of the offshore islands in British Columbia and Baja California. These are recent records in habitat occupancy. This straggling accounts for the occasional record that is picked up at such remote places as Maui in the Hawaiian group.

When the black brant leave their summer and fall habitats in the northland, they follow sky pathways which have been predetermined through past eons. As the southward flight begins, they strike boldly across the north Pacific, and are reported occasionally along the Vancouver Island outer shores. More often they will be seen first in larger numbers along Washington and Oregon ocean shores, working southward with very few entries into the bays and sounds, skimming along the California coast, and finally arriving at the southernmost reaches of Baja California.

The annual southward flight may begin as early as the middle of August or slightly later, and observations suggest that these are the immature birds and perhaps nonbreeding adults. (See Chart 2.) They are reported taking a slightly different course in this southward drift than the breeding birds and will be noted along the shores of the Gulf of Alaska between the Alaskan Peninsula and on the ocean side of the southeastern Alaskan islands. They are reported from such places as Cape St. Elias, Yakutat, and Cape Fairweather; then they swing southward outside of Chichagof and Prince of Wales islands. The earliest

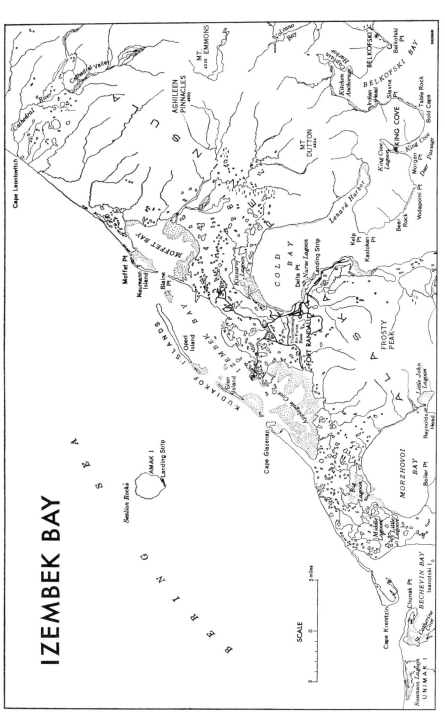

Chart 1. Izembek Bay, just north of Unimak Pass, is a haven of concentration for the southward migration.

arrival on the inland seas is probably reported from Dungeness Bay and Hood Canal, Washington, where I have noted them in mid-October. Usually they remain only a short time and then move southward. In late October I have seen them swimming offshore in the ocean but they rarely venture into harbors such as Grays and Willapa, or Tillamook and Netarts bays on the Oregon coast. Small numbers do come at an early date into Humboldt Bay, northern California. From that point southward they can be seen offshore by ships' crews or passengers along the coast in the usual steamer lanes, or are noted by land observers at such promontories as Pacific Grove, Point Sur, and Point Conception. Laidlaw Williams has a wide series of records in this area. Finally, they reach their usual southern limits in early winter in the lagoons of the lower California peninsula in Mexico.

Because of the isolation of this area, there are very few observers to report their presence, and the dates of arrival and departure are not as well determined as in other portions of their orbit. The first groups reach the Mexican waters in late October or early November, but the height of the concentration does not occur until the last of the southward migrants have left Alaskan areas; the time of their departure from these areas varies greatly each year.

In the southern limits of their flight there is not the same stability in flocks that is found on the summering grounds, and the brant concentrations shift back and forth from one lagoon to another. Areas such as Black Warrior and Scammons lagoons, which are actually connected, have a use pattern of a shifting nature. Flocks from here drift to San Ignacio Lagoon, which lies over a hundred miles southward; smaller segments of the flocks test other lagoons. A very small portion of the aggregate flocks passes beyond Magdalena Bay, which is near the southern tip of the peninsula. In this southern limit of distribution, the restlessness of the birds is not caused by human molestation. Here in this isolated situation the brant are motivated by their own drive, and much of the activity has been observed in early January, continuing as the birds retrace a portion of their southward flight and eventually infiltrate all available habitats both in the quiet waters behind the barrier kelp beds on the California coast and in the lagoons and bays of Oregon, Washington, and the southern coastal areas of Vancouver Island, B.C. At Dungeness and Padilla bays, Hood Canal, and Admiralty Inlet in Washington, and at Boundary Bay, the Gulf of Georgia, and Nootka in British Columbia, they pause for their last loafing period in

Fig. 1. After the hunting season, black brant in British Columbia have become regular shoreside visitors. The fourth brant in the row of five (center foreground) has been identified as an Atlantic brant. (*Photo by E. M. Laing*)

Fig. 2. The breeding brant on the nesting grounds are plump, graceful birds. (*Photo by John Adair*)

Fig. 3. Immature brant have a light grayish edging on their wing coverts. They are nonbreeders. (*Photo by John Adair*)

Fig. 4. The newly hatched goslings are downy balls of soft gray, but swim and run shortly after hatching. (*Photo by John Adair*)

Fig. 5. Brant are gregarious with their kind even when the young are but recently hatched. (*Photo by John Adair*)

Fig. 6. An immature bird, summering near Monterey, California, feeds on eelgrass, the principal food of the brant. (*Photo courtesy of V. Yadon*)

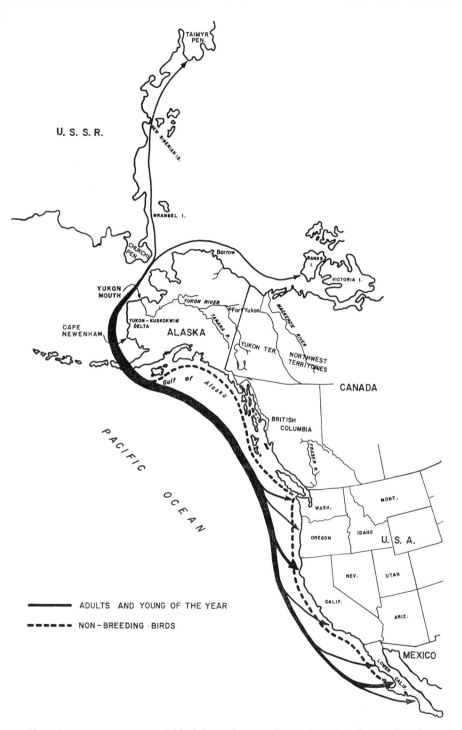

Chart 2. Migration pattern of black brant leaving the northern breeding and molting grounds for their winter rendezvous. Density of lines indicates major flights.

the northern portion of their winter drift. In early April the breeders take off hurriedly, cross the north Pacific, enter the nesting and summering grounds on the sea edge beyond the Aleutian Peninsula, and, in waning numbers, reach the Canadian and Siberian arctic coasts as well, completing their long, narrow orbit.

The references to the inland records reported in the A.O.U. *Checklist* must be recognized as rare instances in these ranges. Reports of this nature coming to my attention during the past thirty years have been prompted solely by the unusualness of the occurrence; most of the birds seemed in distress and their presence there should not be attributed to suitable habitat but rather to some unusual circumstance such as stormy weather on the coast or becoming a chance migrant in a flock of geese of other species.

Robert H. Smith, the U.S. Fish and Wildlife Service Flyway biologist who has made the annual winter flights to enumerate the black brant, revealed in his work in 1958–59 that a small group had visited the west coast of Mexico, almost opposite the lower tip of Baja California and on the east side of the Gulf of California. Dr. and Mrs. Harry G. Plut of Port Townsend, Washington, very familiar with black brant, report seeing a small flock at Acapulco, Mexico, in mid-January, 1960. There may be concentrations in other unexpected places—for example, Price (1899) reported an abundance of brant on the lower Colorado River mouth, particularly at Laguna Salada, but we have no current reports for the area. But it seems unlikely that fluctuations in brant population are caused by large segments of brant eluding the census in successive years.

There are two periods of relative stability of brant numbers in favored habitats. Seven months usually are spent in the northern reaches. The other five months are spent in migration or in the southern range. The greatest concentrations in Mexico (Baja California) are at Scammons and San Ignacio lagoons and Magdalena Bay. Humboldt Bay in California usually holds the greatest late winter concentration of brant in that range. In recent years, few have been found there until February or March. In the vast territory of the northern end of the run, the area between Cape Newenham and the mouth of the Yukon is occupied by the largest segment of nesting or summering brant—with a few of the species nesting perhaps on the Kamchatka coast, dwindling in numbers but with small colonies moving along both the North American and the Siberian arctic coasts to favored spots, usually on the tidal tundra at the mouth of some arctic river or on an island.

ASIAN RECORDS

An extensive search of the records shows that the few black brant seen on the Asiatic coast have been noted with apparent surprise and enthusiasm, even in the early days of observation. Many of these reports were published before 1900, and there is little to indicate that even at that early date any sizable black brant population visited there. Peters (1931) reports that in his search for brant data he found that in winter a few brant reached the western shores of the Pacific, and were noted as far south as Japan and north China.

Attempting to bring into proper focus the present position of the black brant on the Asiatic shores, I resorted to correspondence and addressed a letter to H. Elliott McClure, an American ecologist and currently with the United States Army Medical Research Unit in Malaya. He has traveled widely along the Asiatic shores, and in his letter of May 25, 1958, states, "In the nine years that I have been in this part of the Orient, I have not seen the species and have no information concerning it." McClure suggested that two other naturalists in that area might be of assistance in this search, and he gave me the addresses of Dr. Nagahisa Kuroda of Japan and Mr. C. M. Fennell with the U.S. Forces in Korea. At the same time he thoughtfully addressed letters to these two gentlemen, and in only a few days I received their responses. Said Fennell, "I, personally, have never encountered it in either Japan or Korea and have never seen it brought in by any of the numerous American military hunters during my entire seven and one-half years in Korea and five years in Japan. I have also shown your letter to a friend, Larry Baker, a long-time resident of Korea and an avid hunter. He also claims that he has never seen or bagged the brant in Korea." Referring to Austin's comments on the species in his "Birds of Korea," 1948, Fennell said that Austin had a total of eight specimen records and held that "it is probably best regarded as an uncommon winter visitor." Fennell commented further: "Colonel L. R. Wolfe in his notes on the 'Birds of Korea,' 1950, does not list the species nor does Neff in his 'Birds of Yangdo,' 1956."

This letter was followed in a few days by a welcome letter from Dr.

Kuroda, world famous as a naturalist and a coauthor with O. L. Austin of "Birds of Japan" (1953). Dr. Kuroda made the following comment:

. . . But, recently it appears to have a little increased in Aomori, North Honshiu, as reported by Mr. Mikami. According to his information in Yacho, 21 (2): 124-7, 1956; 24 (1): 50, 1959, the following numbers were counted at Kominato Bay in Aomori:

1954 Kominato	February	ca. :20	(Kiyosu, Tori, 14 [66])
Ominato	December	13	(Mikami, Yacho, 21 [2])
1955 Ominato	January	21	(")
	March	44	
	November	80	(First seen, 2 birds, 1st Nov.)
	December	91	
1958 Ominato	December	70	(Mikami, Yacho, 24 [1])

They are found with wintering flocks of swans, *Cygnus cygnus,* and Mr. Shiro Mikami is now known as the lover of Brant Goose and swans. He is making particular effort for their protection and I would suggest you to write a letter to him for further details.

H. M. Laing of Comox, B.C., who has lived for years on the shore-sides where brant are common visitors in season, reports in a recent letter of a protracted boat trip in 1924:

. . . The main bulk of *nigricans* is on the American side, not the Asiatic. In 1924 I circled around the N. Pacific in a naval trawler—southern Alaska, Aleutian Islands, Attu, Commander Is., the Asiatic side from Petropavlovsk, through the Kuriles to Hokkaido Isl.—April and early May—and I did not see one flock of brant.

It is thought by some that the wide fluctuations in black brant abundance on the North American Pacific coast might result from the birds' drifting toward the Asiatic shores to winter in climates comparable to that of the California and lower California coasts. But this speculation receives little support in the records of these observing people whose interest or careers are closely associated with all species visiting these lands.

In any attempt to discern why brant follow the current circuitous route from nesting to wintering habitats, logic must be cast aside. It would mean a much shorter flight if the birds nesting on the Siberian side drifted down the Kamchatka coast, passed along Korea's shores, and into Japanese waters rather than the one they now follow. Birds nesting on the Bering Sea coast line could likewise shorten their trip to a wintering haven in Asia instead of making the long flight across the North Pacific Ocean and coming to rest in winter in the lagoons of the lower California peninsula. This they do not do.

CASUAL INLAND SIGHTINGS

No mistake is made in identifying the brant as a marine goose. The A.O.U. *Check-list* implies inland records. When you are even a few miles away from the sea edge, the possibility of recording black brant is remote. A search of the records of the West Coast is usually summed up in the following or similar words: "It appears inland or on fresh waters only as a rare straggler." This is a Taverner's (1928) comment, and he continues by indicating only one authenticated record for Manitoba, in all of western Canada. There is little to be learned from a complete search of data on inland sight records since they are few. One was taken in Colorado and one in Texas. Leo K. Couch collected an immature brant on a small pool on Mary's River about three miles from Corvallis, Oregon, in 1918, approximately sixty miles from salt water.

There is a record of a black brant being taken in upper Warner Lakes of Central Oregon at the beginning of the hunting season for waterfowl in 1955. Bryan McNabb, a seasonal employee of the Oregon State Game Commission, observed the bird in the bag of a hunter, and reported that it had been shot while flying with a flock of cacklers. This bird was far inland, approximately 240 miles from the ocean coast. In the following year, 1956, another brant was killed at Crump Lake, about twenty-five miles south of the earlier record area. This bird was identified at a checking station at Warner Lake.

While working in the Sacramento Valley, California, in December, 1934, I noted two taken at a duck pond near Colusa. This was after a severe coastal windstorm, and the complete absence of food in the brant indicated their aversion to any of the available material.

3

Distinctive Characteristics

It is with wonder that a person of normal vision watches a blind man whose face registers complete comprehension as he rapidly presses his fingers over the little raised dots of a Braille manuscript. To a good observer, every species of wildlife has many clear-cut identifying characteristics that are as revealing as the Braille to a blind person.

Wing Structure and Flight Power

A detailed description of their body form and wing structure reveals that the brant are equipped for air-borne life as well as for being at home on the surging ocean, and in their powers of flight they are superior to other geese. Canada geese fly between 36 and 40 miles per hour. Driving an automobile along the Pacific Ocean beach sands, I have clocked black brant at 62 miles per hour. In wingbeat, too, they excel: where the Canada geese usually make two beats per second, brant make between three and four beats in the same time. Body symmetry, the shape of their wings, and their rapid beat signify that they are among the swiftest of the large birds. In addition, the muscle structure of the wing assembly indicates great strength. When these birds can be observed in a storm while other geese are in the air, flight speeds can be compared.

One of the places where their speed can be observed regularly is in the state of Washington, on the waterway dividing the San Juan group of islands from Samish Bay and the mainland on that shore. Here, opposite Eliza, Vendovi, or Guemes islands, the snow geese drifting between their wintering grounds on the Fraser flats of British Columbia and the Skagit River flats of Puget Sound pass back and forth frequently and during all conditions of weather. The black brant spending the night on the Gulf of Georgia usually make a daily trip into Samish and Padilla bays and can often be seen in flight. When the less highly powered snow geese are present, a flock may be in sight for ten to twenty minutes, bucking the prevailing southerly winds. They will be seen quartering back and forth, struggling ponderously against the wind, and following their usual wavy pattern of changing elevations. But the black brant will maintain an almost uniform and level flight above the water as they bore steadily against the wind. Their rapid wingbeats overcome wind resistance and they will pass a point in a fraction of the time necessary for the slower geese. They do not fly high. If the winds are of fifty- to sixty-mile velocity they skim the wave tops, but their speed is uniform and they pass steadily to their feeding grounds, undeterred by gale winds.

FLIGHT MANNERISMS

When flying with their kind, black brant engage in many aerial maneuvers. It is fascinating to see one, two, or a small group, even in the face of a storm, attempting to overtake a mass formation of their fellows, who may be as much as half a mile ahead. A quickening of the wingbeat, a spurt of speed, then the gap begins to close. In still air this might not seem unusual because, as the space between the two groups is rapidly shortened, the swiftly moving wings of the trailing birds convey impressions of considerable effort. In a severe storm it does not seem so simple; yet the trailing birds quickly overcome the gap between them and their fellows in spite of winds of thirty to forty miles an hour, and when overtaking their rivals may find themselves with such momentum that they must engage in rapid maneuvers to adjust to the speed of the group.

An interesting pattern which is not common to other geese or waterfowl also develops on places like Izembek Bay, where as many as ten thousand brant may be seen in flight at one time. Against a sunset sky one may see long strings of brant, but they seem to be using parallel tracks. They undulate in flight and rise and fall almost in unison. This type of flight is more often observed on a calm day when sudden wind gusts and updrafts do not prevail. In the still air, as many as twenty or thirty formations flying parallel to each other may be seen heading for the same rendezvous. They arrive there with clamorous greetings for each other, settle down, gabble excitedly for a few minutes, and then become almost motionless. This is what hunters mean when they refer to "rafts" of black brant, an indication of the gregariousness of the species.

The black brant is truly an exile from the land, clinging to the restless seas with the devotion of an oceanic bird. The struggle to remain land-free is persistent. They are rarely seen flying to shelter as a storm builds up. Even after long winter nights of howling storms, morning seldom finds the black brant in the constricted waters where other waterfowl have been driven to shelter. The boatman or the coast guardsman braving the sea finds them scattered, ranging the waves, swimming valiantly to the topmost crest, and sliding down the far side. All this time they are gleaning tidbits of food in the perpetual battle for life.

FEATHER WEAR

Among the brant in the hunter's bag in late fall or early winter, and in museum specimens collected at that time of the year, the wing and tail feathers evidence excessive flight wear. Because of the season, it must be presumed that the birds have had only the migratory flight from the nesting to the feeding grounds; other geese, whose flights are mostly inland, show far less feather wear at this time of year. The faster wingbeat and speed of flight are apparently a factor in the brant's condition; there is also the fact that the black brant are in the air more often and for longer daily flights than other geese. The only comparable wear among ducks is found in the ruddies, the scaups, and the diving birds, which use their tail feathers frequently in landing. Birds like the mallard and the pintail do not show a similar degree of wear, since their practice of dropping into the water without persistently using their tails as a water drag more often leaves their feathers unmarred.

In collecting specimens for the museum, birds taken shortly after their molt would be in perfect or "mint" condition (to borrow a term from book or gun experts). Brant that winter on the northern end of their migratory range often attain complete and unmarred breeding plumage before starting the journey back to their nesting grounds.

WARINESS

Because of its gregarious tendencies, the black brant is often said to be a foolish bird that decoys readily. In truth it is extremely wary, but has a tenacious tie to its kind. Where decoys are placed so they are easily seen or a large number of decoys are used, and if the hunter is skilled in calling brant, the situation is almost irresistible to one or two birds, or to a small passing flock. When the hunting season is on, there are

only a few sanctuaries near the shore where brant are safe from humans. These are spots that furnish sand and loafing space, which are usually on promontories, sand bars, or islands. They are becoming increasingly scarce. Few such places exist in wintering habitats naturally and those available are often subject to human intrusion. On the nesting grounds of the North, from the mouth of the Kuskokwim to the farthest reach of nesting activity on the arctic coast, brant are continually alert to the human, particularly if he seems to be carrying a gun. One gunshot will also arouse a babble from the entire population on a concentration ground. In the vast concentrations of Izembek Bay, one shot on a calm day may disturb the thousands feeding on eelgrass beds two or three miles away. Recognizing the hazard, they will take wing, often going to the farthermost reach of the bay.

Black brant do not afford "potshots" for they do not drift in on a flooding tide to the beach side, as ducks do. Their food usually lies offshore. If undisturbed, pintails and teal may feed during the incoming tide in a shallow bay to the driftwood's edge. Not so with brant.

The only place where they may become vulnerable is some head-land—if it is low and juts far out into the sea—where they may string across. More often they are skimming at the edge of the open sea or across mid-bay. This is why people, even natives of a maritime district, rarely know much of the black brant and see them so seldom that they usually confuse them with cormorants, which may be seen daily in many marine areas. The hunters, however, know the favored places where brant become vulnerable in flight or where they approach to loaf and procure grit. Decoys at such a spot often permit a limit take for many guns, especially on stormy days when gun noise is muted.

VOICE AND CALLS

It is impossible to describe with words the various calls of the brant so that a person hearing its voice for the first time could identify its origin. Neither can these calls be repeated accurately by the human voice until one is completely familiar with the vocabulary of the wild brant. This is because the individual pitch and timbre of the human voice varies so that it may take considerable practice to imitate the bird's wild call. The successful brant caller usually performs this feat by placing the tip of his tongue lightly near the first ridge above the point where the teeth meet the gums. The sound that more nearly imitates the brant vocabulary in this phase of the call can be represented in these letters, *tiurr-r tiurr-r, tiurr-r tiurr-r,* and is accomplished by forcing air from the mouth against the tongue until it vibrates rapidly. The most common call is made up of two notes, one high and one low. This, done in the pitch of the brant, often attracts the birds to a stool of decoys.

An intruder on the nesting ground will be scolded persistently by the brant in the air, which invariably include the mate of the nesting bird and often a scattered flight of restless and irritated companions. These will continually issue a deep-throated grunt while flying, in a restrained way, hovering above the intruder as though they are about to alight. They are timid enough, however, so that this rarely occurs except at a distance; but the continual, threatening call rings over the tundra and alerts more and more brant. The intrusion, which with other birds might stir only the molested pair, is a community affair in a black brant colony and many rally to the defense of those who seem to be in jeopardy.

They are relentless in hazing an intruder from their nesting grounds. In the summer of 1957, while concealed at a considerable distance, I observed such a melee among a colony of black brant. It developed that a fox was plodding along, paying little attention to the brant. During its entire course, as long as it was crossing their immediate domain and until it disappeared into the higher vegetation inland from the nesting area, the fox was accompanied by scolding birds.

When the goslings are hatched the parents continually show their great devotion. When close at hand you can hear them murmuring or whispering of either warning or fear if they are pressed. This often happens when a naturalist attempts to take close-up camera shots or approaches for other reasons. Both birds will hiss, which is the only sound they make which suggests they might be related to the other geese of the genus *Branta*.

The common and often-repeated calls of the brant vary greatly from those of other species. The larger members of the *Brantas,* such as the Canadas, have a harsh, unmusical call. This can be imitated by scraping a piece of slate stone against a thin-walled and resonant sound box to achieve volume. Many commercial goose calls are made on this principle. Brant hunters have tried with some success to imitate this device, but it must be daintily made with a thin-sided sound box even to approach a sound that might resemble the brant's call.

In migration the black brant do not fly at heights usually favored by other geese. The late Charles Gropstis, an arctic flyer, often reported sighting southbound Canada geese at eight to ten thousand feet in the Mackenzie River basin during the fall migration. Although brant may swing up and down, changing elevation from near the ocean's surface to heights of two or three hundred feet, their usual flight is but a little above the ocean. While this is happening, you hear very little of the birds unless you are concealed nearby, and then you can hear soft murmurings that mean little to you but are sounds of apparent contentment. In them one hears nothing of fear or warning.

At the outset of a long flight to their nesting grounds, you will hear a continuous clamor of considerable duration among the multitude of scattered birds on the water and then when the flock rises, usually in the still of evening, there is a roar, followed by an excited gabbling for a short while. If you happen to be a mile or two from the point of their rise and they approach in steady rapid flight, you may hear soft murmurings as they cross over, heading on their long flight toward their summer home. But this sound is quickly swallowed up by distance as they speed northward.

In all my years of observation, even in storm-tossed areas where the brant are numerous, I have never heard them call wildly in the dead of night or long after darkness with the same clamor that signals departure from their wintering waters. Resident flocks in winter may resort to the eelgrass beds, but the only noises you may hear are those lesser mutterings of feeding in the periods of long tidal runout. Since these birds are very gregarious, it is the daily rallying calls on still days when they are feeding or loafing that you hear most often.

Brant calls do not sound like those of other geese. The Canadas, especially when they utter calls of warning, open their bills wide. On the nesting grounds of the brant there are many chances to see several species of geese intermingled. The noisiest of all, and the most easily irritated, are those of the emperor family. In contrast to the quiet secretiveness of the black brant, the emperor will begin scolding when a man is half a mile away. Its high-pitched call can be easily heard at great distances. It is common to see an emperor in the nesting area standing on a hummock or a bank edge, silhouetted against the sky, scolding endlessly or calling its young, even though they may be very near at hand. This it does in a most raucous way.

Black brant do not follow this pattern of irritation, reserving their voices for more apparent crises; and when they do call, they do not open their bills in the gaping manner of the emperors. In captivity, both immature and adult brant have been closely watched when calling: they seem to do it with ease, yet the sound carries well. Rarely is a flock of brant heard in the far distance when in flight. The hunter must be alert when the birds are flying since they can come in on quiet wings and pass by swiftly. There is little warning of their presence as they approach, but they may be heard in hushed murmurings as they pass near at hand. However, singles or small bands coming into a flock, or over decoys, do engage in lusty and salutatory greetings.

But black brant are not stolid or expressionless. A mated pair, being joined by their young, often begin a spirited exchange of soft sibilant noises with much bowing and swaying of the body and neck, almost sweeping the ground with their heads. But you do not see the gaping open bill so common to the more voluble members of the goose family.

LONGEVITY

Since there have been so few brant geese harbored in captivity for long periods of time, it is difficult to trace the life span of the bird or estimate its prospects of natural survival. A study of the retained egg follicles and the few instances of brant in captivity lead to the conclusion that life span is long. Wesley Batterson, a naturalist employed by the Oregon State Game Department, and members of his family held captive black brant for approximately eight years. At the end of that time, the birds were in good condition and appeared to have a life span considerably longer than was estimated.

Since the brant are quite adaptable in captivity and after as little as a week's confinement will readily take grain, particularly wheat, with a combination of green stuff such as lettuce, alfalfa, and clover, they are quite content and remain in good physical condition. It is heartening that this is so with several of the wild forms. It is actually insurance that the species can never become extinct; if retained in a few places, many species could be perpetuated. Not only would it be useful to retain them so their stock would be available, but in observing them, their needs and habits could be determined so that our management would be based on knowledge rather than on supposition.

4

Feeding Habits

Unlike most other waterfowl, the brant do not include a wide variety of both plant and animal matter in their diet. Food samples obtained from various sources give supporting evidence to observations that brant persistently utilize only a few key species, particularly eelgrass (see Figs. 6, 7) and sea lettuce.

SOURCES OF FOOD

Food samples for nutritional study and evaluation were gathered over a considerable range. Colleagues in wildlife work, Robert Corthell of Coos Bay, Wesley Batterson of Nehalem, Oregon, and William Q. Wick of Conway, Washington, kindly provided additional samples.

A further and significant contribution came from the California State Game Department through the efforts of Howard R. Leach, in charge of their efficient food laboratory. This included a helpful number of scats from Alaska and California.

In addition to the food samples, gizzards collected by U.S. Fish and Wildlife Service over a considerable period of time were analyzed by Leach and Browning of the California game staff. These samples lend supporting evidence to the observations that brant persistently utilize only a few key species. Eelgrass and sea lettuce have appeared in both the gizzards and scats of the brant throughout the range where they could be collected. Unfortunately, work of this nature could not be carried out at the time of my visit to Scammons Lagoon in the Mexican territory, because most of the plane flights into that area were with land planes. Pilots have been very hesitant to land, even with amphibious planes, on the water areas where collections could be made because the shortage of fresh water there would make it impossible to neutralize the effects of the salt on the plane by a good washdown. Flights to areas where an air base might have water facilities would entail long trips in Mexico.

In a detailed study of the food demands of a wildlife species, there is usually a considerable list of preferred foods and a need for detailed analysis of the food-habitat relationship. In many areas, an imbalance of one or another is often the difference between extinction and survival for some species. In the case of the black brant, such an approach can be greatly simplified because of the list of their preferred foods is extremely short, with all evidence pointing to eelgrass, usually *Zostera marina,* and sea lettuce, *Ulva* sp., which is usually found in the black brant's orbit to be *Ulva lactuca, Ulva taeniata,* or *Ulva linza.* H. K. Phinney, associate professor at Oregon State University, who is familiar with the Pacific coast sea lettuce beds, says that, of these, *Ulva lactuca* is by far the most abundant and most conspicuous form. The presence of eelgrass or sea lettuce indicates a potentially suitable habitat. When these foods are in abundance and growing in a locality acceptable to the mature brant, their need for sustenance is thus met by only two preferred foods.

Unlike most other waterfowl, their diet does not include a wide variety of both plant and animal matter. Any animal matter taken is in the nature of incidental food items borne on the favored vegetation. This includes such forms as the diatoms, the bryozoans, the gastropods, fish eggs, shrimp, and, from the evidence at hand, an occasional insect. From their trace occurrence, these items are apparently ingested simply because they are attached to the vegetable forms. In percentage of volume or value, they probably contribute very little to the sustenance of the brant. To fishermen who are critical of brant on herring spawning grounds where eelgrass may be covered with herring eggs, this statement may seem an oversimplification, but it must be remembered that the brant may be in this situation for only a few days in some years and not at all in others, nor during the hunting season.

The nutritional value of eelgrass and sea lettuce, indicated by crude protein content, proves adequate for good health. Brant utilizing these two foods are almost universally in excellent physical condition. An analysis of crude protein values has shown that the Izembek Bay eelgrass samples (Table 2) have about half the value of those in Washington and Oregon (7.35 per cent: 14.74 per cent). Yet we know that the Alaska area is the conditioning area of both the adults and immature brant, preparing them physically for the long ocean flight to their wintering grounds. This should be convincing proof that the preferred

TABLE 2

CRUDE PROTEIN LEVEL DETERMINATIONS OF FOOD SAMPLES*
(A Test for Relative Food Value)

SAMPLES	NUMBER	COLLEC-TION DATE	Na PER CENT	CRUDE PROTEIN	
				Per cent	Average
Eelgrass (*Zostera marina*)					
Alaska					
Izembek Bay	#1	9-16-59	4.60	5.37	—
Izembek Bay	#2	9-18-59	4.10	9.34	7.35
Washington					
Padilla Bay	#3	2-14-59	4.00	13.02	—
Port Townsend	#4	1-25-59	5.52	12.65	—
Willapa Bay	#5	2-20-59	3.94	18.55	14.74
Oregon					
Tillamook Bay	#6	1-19-59	4.24	14.11	—
Netarts Bay	#7	1-19-59	3.08	15.94	—
Coos Bay	#8			14.65	14.9
California					
Humboldt Bay	#9	1- 4-59	5.08	8.76	—
Humboldt Bay	#10	1- 4-59	5.08	14.65	—
Humboldt Bay	#11	12-20-58	6.00	12.44	—
Morro Bay	#12	1- 2-59	4.10	8.21	—
Tomales Bay	#13	1- 3-59	6.00	14.68	11.74
Sea Lettuce (*Ulva*)					
Bolinas Bay, California		7- 3-59	2.66	11.95	—
Bolinas Bay, California		—	—	14.68	—
Waldport Bay, Oregon		—	—	14.65	—

* Oregon Cooperative Wildlife Research Unit, Analysis by Department of Agricultural Chemistry, Oregon State College.

foods are by themselves an adequate diet. Our concern should be to protect, by every means, the key supplies of the species in their preferred habitats; to insure the black brant enough sanctuary areas so their natural inclinations are satisfied; and to remember that the brant as a species could be wiped out within a few years unless these desperate needs are supplied. We have had examples of a crisis pressing brant on our Atlantic coast when disease almost removed eelgrass from their wintering waters.

Brant have been observed mixing with other birds in some areas where their food is scarce. This may be due to storms, or to persistently high tides during the winter daylight hours, with very short runouts at night, so that eelgrass beds are not exposed to feeding brant. Continued molestation also restricts normal feeding. The combined handicaps can leave brant hungry. If so, they may follow the scaup, the scoters, or the golden-eyes during the daylight periods when the latter

Harold Cramer Smith

are foraging on the submerged coastal shelves and tidelands. The diving ducks, in their hasty garnering of shellfish or mollusks from the bottom, often bring eelgrass or sea lettuce to the surface. With amazing accuracy, the black brant anticipate the emergence of the diving birds, and are usually surprisingly close to the point of their hosts' reappearance. If the quest is successful, they are quick to grasp any vegetative tidbits that may be attached to the duck's sea-bottom harvest. These morsels are of little moment to the diving ducks, who are seeking animal foods, but they mean food to the hungry brant. They persist in following the divers and many times the reward is important. I have often observed this on Puget Sound, Hood Canal, and the Strait of Juan de Fuca.

When feeding, the black brant may scatter over a wide area and do not progress as canvasbacks do, in a tight flotilla, moving forward in one direction. On stormy days, when gleaning from the tide edge, they

usually face into the wind and the onrushing waves. They cruise back
and forth, alert for even small particles of food.

FOOD DEMAND AND FEEDING

The vigorous life led by the black brant indicates a high food demand, and this is substantiated by observations on the feeding
grounds. Studies of this kind can be best made after a hunting season
is closed and there is little danger of molesting the birds of the sea.
Brant will be active at many stages of tide during the daylight hours,
particularly when the low tides fall in hours of darkness and they are
denied the uncovered eelgrass beds. It is at these times that they will
be seen swimming above the eelgrass beds which they apparently anticipate will be exposed to them later. They are aware that fronds can
be found drifting to the surface from time to time, though in short
supply. These remnants are avidly taken. At high tide I have noted the
birds feeding persistently for as long as three hours with hardly a
pause.

Their digestion is very rapid and thorough, and if you find their
loafing bars, such as at the entrance to Izembek Bay, Alaska, or the
various sandspits up and down the coast, you will see an abundance of
scats quite out of proportion to the number of birds that are visiting
these areas. Likewise, if you happen to be in an anchored boat down
bay from a good-sized flock of brant, you will soon notice the well-
formed scats floating by in large numbers. At a little distance they will
remind you of green caterpillars. Observing them closely you will find
that most of the chlorophyll and succulent substance of the plant have
been consumed. Only the tougher plant tissues and fibers remain. Because of this the scats will be buoyant and float readily.

Their rapid digestion explains why the brant are such avid feeders,
continually gorging themselves on their favorite food for hours at a
time. In early March, as the birds come close inshore and are frightened only by the most aggressive intruder, they can be watched close
at hand. Once I saw a single bird eat fifteen pieces of green sea lettuce—each piece almost the size of a human hand—in only a few moments. This material is very thin but the bulk in substance was considerable. After such an indulgence one would presume that the bird
would have been satisfied. This was not true. It continued to forage
aggressively.

There is little comparison between the food substance taken by the ducks and that taken by the black brant. The food of puddle ducks is quite substantial. It will consist of tubers, mollusks, crustacea, seeds, grasses, and grains made up of firm material. With the black brant this is not so. The edible material is mostly succulents.

Since the extreme low tides are more frequent during the gloom of early evening or after darkness in winter, the brant's daylight search for food is continual. When the hunting season is on, and for several weeks after it ends, black brant cannot utilize all of the potential feeding area because they are still intimidated by gun pressure. Confidence returns, however, as they find they are unmolested, and it is then that they come near the shore line and feed actively. They are more successful in feeding when waves are stirring up fronds and leaves from the bottom in shallow water. This type of feeding is more productive than the open-sea foraging which must be their lot during the winter months.

The brant are comfortable on stormy seas, and this indifference to rough waters remains whether they are on the open ocean or in the choppy seas on the inland reaches. On April 5, 1959, a sudden southwest storm of high velocity hit the Washington coast, and gusts ranging up to sixty and seventy miles an hour struck the Strait of Juan de Fuca and Hood Canal. On that day approximately 400 birds were feeding along the shore line near Jorstad Creek, Hood Canal. Brant here fed greedily, oblivious of the storm.

Eelgrass Disease—Its Influence on Food

Infestations in eelgrass, which have created widespread losses, particularly on the Atlantic tidal waters, are due to the mycetozoan Labyrinthula. This organism lives in the leaves of the eelgrass and causes the plant to waste away, probably by absorbing into itself the vital fluids and substances of the plant. In the areas where this parasite is rampant and the eelgrass is heavily affected, it may recover something of its former abundance after a few years. The plant is very firm-rooted, and there may be some possibility that a regrowth occurs, although there is little at the present time to verify this statement. The fruiting buds, however, are numerous in healthy eelgrass fronds, and wave and water action could quickly redistribute these bodies as a potential source of new plants. The combination of surviving plants and

new growth has partially restored many of the ravaged beds but only
to the point where they offer a minimum supply for the brant. In the
few areas where the concentrations of black brant occur, any agent
that would destroy the bulk of the growing plants could seal their
doom.

5

Mating Activities

It has long been known that most geese when mated are seemingly inseparable, at least during the time of the year when they are responsible for building their nests, laying eggs, hatching the young, and bringing up the brood. In the species that take long migratory flights, the mated birds have the ability to remain together even where the aerial pathways lead through dark nights, snowstorms, fog, and every vicissitude of weather. In spite of the added hazards of mankind's disturbance, many do arrive safely at the nesting grounds with the unswerving purpose of perpetuating their kind. In the light of this knowledge, management restraints on decimating factors insure surprising yields in waterfowl in most years.

It has been generally accepted that the Canada geese mate for life. Only when one of the pair is lost will the other seek a second mate. Sufficient evidence supports this idea of association in the many instances of captive or observable geese, which have taken up a more or less fixed habitat or by some physical characteristic have been easily identified. Gabrielson and Jewett (1940) in *Birds of Oregon* write that Canada geese "mate for life and nesting begins early."

It is not known definitely that the black brant follow the same habits though this seems probable. Their mating procedures distinguish them from other geese. Since the brant are remarkably proficient in flight, it is not surprising that some of the activities of mate selection occur aloft; and the air-borne chase of the usual trio, which marks the beginning of the season of choosing a mate, is an exhibition of aerial acrobatics that would be the envy of a flight exhibition team of the Armed Forces.

MATING SEASON

Mating does not begin on the nesting grounds. It begins on the wintering waters, perhaps several thousands of miles from the place where the brant will build their nests. Only rarely will they remain in the vicinity of their wintering area and attempt to nest. This happens when injuries or other circumstances impairing flight prevent them from returning to the arctic sod that gave them birth. There are records of this on Tomales and Humboldt bays in California, and in other areas along the Pacific coast states. In 1958 a pair produced a brood of five and raised them to maturity on the Oregon coast. It was reported by Robert Corthell, an Oregon State game biologist stationed at Coos Bay, Oregon, who found their nesting site on an arm of the bay. A fisherman of the area informed Corthell that this was the second year they had been there. It was apparent that the goose was crippled. James Moffitt told me of a similar instance on Tomales Bay in the early 1930's, and reported that the goose was crippled.

In observing the ducks at mating time, one usually notes a period of displays, particularly by the males, when the early surge of interest comes with the waning of winter. This is particularly noticeable on calm, bright, warm days, and most of the activity is on the water, with short flights in the immediate vicinity of the favored duck. These actions finally develop into the activity of several birds and the eventual choosing of a mate by the female. Brant mating begins earlier, in January or early February; at this time the birds are usually at the southern end of the migration, and the climate is very much like late winter in more northerly waters, where the ducks carry out their mating antics and maneuvers. In mid-January, 1958, trios of mating brant were noted in flight in California at Mission Bay, San Diego, Morro Bay, and as early as February 27 and 28 on Dungeness Bay in the state of Washington, and on March 27 near Belfair on Hood Canal.

Brant, unlike ducks, do not mature in their first year; in addition, many in the brant flock have mated in previous years. For these reasons, fewer brant than ducks are stirred each year by the mate selection urge. Because brant of the year do not mate, but must wait the third year or later for maturity, there will be only a few reaching the physical condition that forecasts the mating venture (see Fig. 8).

If a large raft of brant are at their ease in mid-bay on some calm, clear, warm mid-winter day, you may see a group of three rise from the waters and start a series of aerial maneuvers and pursuits that is highly unusual. You see very little sign of mating action or display by the birds on the water. The preliminary steps do not seem to partake of the same aggressive pattern of the ducks. You are alert to the activity mainly when several birds rise into the air and fly off at high speed, making erratic changes in course. They fly in a wide circle that encompasses many miles, swinging back into the vicinity of the flock on the waters below, but often continuing the chase for ten or fifteen minutes. It appears that the goose is in the lead and the birds following are usually two or more competing ganders, who swing back

and forth in erratic flight, demonstrating their great ability by plunging from right to left and carrying out a series of aerial maneuvers that display their unusual flying skill and power. The aerial chase ends eventually, after this series of sweeping flights at an elevation of three or four hundred feet above the water; the birds glide down gracefully and join the raft and no further bold demonstration seems to take place as the birds rest and relax with their fellows. The chase, however, may be repeated.

If the concentration of brant is large, these nuptial flights may be seen many times during the day, but they are few in relation to the entire flock. Evidence of mated birds, however, is common when they feed close to shore. If two mated brant are approached by a third bird, the intruder will receive a sharp peck if he ventures too close.

The bond between mates holds them together from the eelgrass beds of Scammons Lagoon in Baja California to the sedge grass tidelands at the mouth of the Kashunuk on the Bering Sea.

When the paired birds reach the northernmost late wintering

grounds in Oregon, Washington, and British Columbia they are at the height of beauty. Their next venture must obviously be one of importance.

Under the regulations for harvesting black brant, which permit heavy pressures on the mass of birds leaving the wintering grounds in Mexico, mated birds are exposed to great danger. They are always the first sizable group to arrive at the hunting grounds of the northwest states and British Columbia; thus they may be pressed by the gunner at a highly critical time. Qualified observers on the Alaskan Peninsula and the Kuskokwim-Yukon nesting areas report the presence of mated birds in mid-April, and by early May it is obvious that most of the nesting birds have arrived. This varies somewhat with the season, however, for in some years the hatches are complete quite early and in others late. For example, our observations on the Kashunuk flats in 1957 indicated that they had arrived quite early. The height of the hatch had occurred before our arrival on June 17. Site selection, nest building, egg laying, and incubation require approximately forty to forty-five days' time, and this would mean that the paired birds had been active in the area in late April or at the latest in the first days of May, but before that had made the long aerial journey probably from as far south as Magdalena Bay in Baja California. Hunting, which in that year was permitted till late January in the United States or into February in Canada, might therefore destroy or divide a pair as they progressed northward up the coast. To increase this practice of a delayed hunting season, extending it further into the early spring, may jeopardize the survival of black brant.

There are sufficient records to show that those brant which could not produce young on the northern nesting grounds may remain along the Pacific coast into early summer; immature or unmated birds fall into this class. This is particularly true in such areas as the Strait of Juan de Fuca and Boundary Bay in Washington, and even into the reaches stretching up toward Olympia and along the Gulf of Georgia shores in British Columbia. In *Birds of Washington State* (1953) Jewett reports: "On June 21, 1940, Jewett watched 12 brants feeding in the 'lagoon' on the Dungeness National Wildlife Refuge. It is assumed that these were nonbreeders that failed to go north as is the normal habit of the species." There is little doubt that the brant on the nesting grounds of the subarctic, particularly, represent a large segment of the entire black brant population. It is also noticeable that a high percentage of these birds are not nesting birds.

CROSSBREEDING

During migration, various subspecies of brant often intermingle. *Nigricans* mix with *bernicla bernicla* on the Siberian Arctic coast, and some of them occupy the same breeding range with *hrota* in the eastern limits of their range, north of the Canadian Arctic mainland in such places as Prince Patrick Island (Handley, 1950). There are unauthenticated reports of hybridizing in these common summering grounds, but little evidence of this afield or in present museum specimens is found. Hybridized birds are few or almost nonexistent. Why?

The answer seems to be that mate choosing occurs long before the brant leave their wintering range. By the time they arrive at the breeding grounds, most of the birds are already mated and copulation completed. Thus the fervor of selecting a mate and consummating reproduction when they meet brant of another subspecies in the northland is probably rare indeed. If this had not always been true of the brant, there would now be so many crosses that, instead of calling them *hrota, nigricans,* or *bernicla,* we could classify all the brant as simply one group.

It is to be noted that when a pair of Atlantic brant comes to the Pacific coast the paired birds are generally inseparable; and if the evidence were sought out in the case of western black brant stragglers to the Atlantic shores, a similar situation would perhaps be noted. A pair of captive Atlantic brant at large with unmated black brant showed no disposition to favor any of the latter group. These birds, held pinioned in Wesley Batterson's spacious enclosure for three years, consistently remained aloof from the black brant.

NESTING GROUND ACTIVITY

These are memorable days of the early spring, when the traditional nesting grounds are again alive with brant activity. But the brant are not alone. The mink and the weasel appear with bright eyes, as the nesting birds once more return to give these animals a land of plenty. The selection of nesting territory by black brant is obviously influenced by their devotion to surging sea. Although the vast tract of lowland between the mouth of the Yukon and the Kuskokwim is ideal nesting habitat and well occupied by the puddle ducks like the pintail, the divers like the eider, the old squaws, and several species of geese, black brant do not join them in the common pattern of nesting ground selection. The portion they choose is actually a very narrow fringe—a sea-edge strip usually only a mile or so in width and rarely more than five miles from the open sea. It is near a river, estuary, or slough. Most of it is vulnerable to the fluctuating levels of Bering Sea and is occasionally inundated by the run-off from the rivers that intersect this alluvial plain.

A nest of Pacific black brant containing four eggs was taken by the Russian Polar Expedition on July 6, 1903, at Faddejefski Island. Birula, according to Pleske (1928), found nesting birds on the islands of New Siberia, and it is noteworthy that the black brant should select nesting sites in an area so like the Bering Sea ocean edge. In this work, Pleske comments on the fact that *Branta bernicla bernicla,* the brant wintering in northern Europe, prefer to nest in the higher parts of the Taimyr Peninsula, placing their nests among the boulders or broken rock that cover the ground there. In the archipelago of New Siberia, on the other hand, the black brant nest in the low areas covered with standing water, on the shores of rivers and lakes not far from the sea coast. This is an exact description of the nesting habitat of the black brant along the Alaskan shores. The few specimens taken by the Siberian expedition add to the accuracy of the identification, making the combined information irrefutable.

The first few days on the nesting grounds are a time of rest for the black brant. This occurrence has been described by observers such as Robert Jones, who each spring have seen the brant drifting in from their long-ranging and wearisome flight from British Columbia or the Pacific coastal states. There is little doubt that the birds' flight across the North Pacific includes few breaks or resting periods, for they arrive at the Alaskan Peninsula very soon after leaving their southern range and they are weary.

After this short period of inertia the brant select a site for the nests they will build. They do not hurry, for the days are long, the search for food is not confining, and the birds course back and forth over the nesting grounds with considerable time for resting. In this area of numerous ponds and lakes you can see where the birds have sat hour after hour, for they have practically destroyed the vegetation on their favored pond edges. Their excreta exercises a control of all vegetation, so that for a distance of a foot or two around a pond edge, and in many instances encircling the small ponds, the bare ground is exposed.

As a nest site the black brant will often select small islands in a pond containing a few square feet of territory, or choose a little promontory extending into one of these ponds or lakes. The promontory is a fine vantage point for watching the approach of enemies. Although some sites give the nesting brant almost complete protection from land approach, the birds usually take the precaution of facing the direction from which the danger might come. Then they can escape by slipping off into the water or taking wing. Brant take advantage of a depression in the ground in choosing a nest site and there is some evidence that they actually scoop out the earth to make a provision for concealment. Some nests are found in conspicuous places, though the sites with escape facilities usually dominate.

The observation that brant seem to take advantage of natural depressions, or in some manner obtain the right type of base for their nest, can be supported by other evidence which indicates that they are capable of forming a proper base themselves. In commenting on the captive brant held by the Wildfowl Trust at Slimbridge, Gloucester, England, S. T. Johnstone, curator of the Trust, reports in a letter to the author that brant procured from James Elliott of Oregon, originating from eggs collected in Alaska, showed signs of nesting in their third year of captivity. When one pair was struck by the nesting urge they showed that they were able to make what Mr. Johnstone terms a "scrape," obviously a depression in the lawn in the eleven-acre enclosure which has been set aside for the many brant held there. This could well be the procedure of the Alaska brant in their native habitat, but I have never had the opportunity to see this operation. Many of the nests found in Alaska, either when occupied or after abandonment, showed this typical situation.

When the birds nest on flat ground the nests always seem to be such that the sitting bird is exposed very little above the ground level. With the goose's habit of laying her head on the ground with neck outstretched, concealment is often effective.

They build a beautiful nest (see Fig. 9). It is lined with fine grasses which, because of the heat of the bird's body, are almost always well dried and cured when found. This is true even where winter has removed most vestiges of last year's grasses. Signs of soiling, mold, or decay are rarely obvious after incubation has begun. Upon this foundation, they place layers of down. This is taken from the goose, and there is little evidence that the gander is associated with this activity. The brant, like other waterfowl, have abundant special down on the breast and underbody, grown just previous to nesting. The brant's use of this material is far more extensive than in most other species.

During the nesting time the removal of down causes no noticeable change in the goose's appearance, for she does not need to use any feathers. There is enough down to make a good blanket for covering the eggs, which the goose carefully does whenever she withdraws to feed. In the hunting season following the nesting season, when the goose has had an opportunity to restore in part the down used in nest building, one can hardly see the area of heavy depletion. Plucking off the breast feathers exposes the down: it is a solid mat and under the hand feels like fur. The increased growth of down at nesting time explains why the nest can be so abundantly lined.

The weather at the time of nesting can periodically become quite cold and raw, and in parts of the nesting range freezing temperatures are not unusual. The abundant use of down has two effects: it provides a good cushion and blanket to exclude the cold, especially from the edges of the nest; and it places the warm breast of the bird in much closer contact with the eggs than if the heavy natural blanket of down still remained on the incubating goose. This is particularly important in an area of such temperature ranges. It has been found in our works with other nesting birds, the Chinese pheasant for instance, that a sudden wave of cold air, the kind that might come with a late spring windstorm, may cause a temperature drop of from twenty to thirty degrees in a few hours. This is quickly reflected in the heat that the incubating bird delivers to the eggs. In the case of pheasants, a drop from 99°F. to 72°F. in four hours during a windstorm has been recorded. This phenomenon, which occurs often, was recorded on a thermograph by means of an electric thermocouple, measuring accurately inner egg temperatures. These experiments were repeated many times in the relatively mild climate of Oregon. On the Arctic coast even more severe fluctuations can be expected. Hence, with the removal of breast down, the body warmth of the nesting brant is more directly applied to the eggs, and embryo survival, unless temperatures are extremely low, is insured. In the instance of the pheasant studies, the twenty-seven degree drop did not affect egg hatchability.

An incubating goose presses close upon her nest and there are no signs of visible eggs; since she appears to be sheltering them perfectly, it is assumed that all is well. She may, however, suffer greatly from the cold, and other birds in similar conditions have often abandoned their eggs.

Watching nesting pheasants in the research study area on Eliza Island, Washington, where the temperature dipped down to fifty degrees or below on many days, I saw that the sitting hen was extremely uncomfortable. Only her persistence and devotion to her duty protected the eggs sufficiently so that a normal hatch resulted. The black brant's extra precautions in nest building allow her to cope quite successfully with the hazards of the northern nesting grounds, but there must be times when even these natural safeguards are insufficient and optimum levels of reproduction are probably the exception.

Gillham, reporting on Canadian Arctic conditions, wrote as follows of an experience at the mouth of the Mackenzie River on the Canadian Arctic coasts:

This year the birds appeared at about their usual time and went into the nesting ground. About eight days after the migration a severe freeze came on. Water areas were entirely frozen over. Almost immediately, the birds abandoned their nesting on the coast and returned within the delta where open water could be had. Here they remained for several days until the frozen lakes and streams again thawed out.

The result of this freeze on the nesting ground was apparent. Egg clutches were smaller, hatching was delayed two weeks, nests were almost devoid of down, the first nesting attempt having utilized most of this insulating material. Some nests of two stories were found. The first deposit of eggs was found in the lower part of the structure, then the second nests were built upon the top of the old ones. Eggs were found scattered at random all over the nesting ground. Large nests were noted with as many as thirteen eggs, or three times the size of a normal one. Predatory birds were attracted in great numbers by the abandoned eggs and nests. The whole procedure of a normal nesting year was disrupted.

Concrete evidence of the effect of this sudden freezing spell is found in the record on size of egg clutches, which Gillham provides (see Table 3). Gillham also noted brood sizes for 1951, 1953, and 1954, respectively, as 3.4, 2.8, and 2.01.

NUMBER OF EGGS LAID

Henry Hansen and Urban Nelson (1957) have given us the data on 116 brant nests. The average for the total number was 3.5 eggs per clutch. Of the observed young remaining from 42 broods, there was a decrease from 3.8 young at hatching time to 3.2 young per brood in less than a month.

C. E. Gillham (1940) discovered black brant nesting near the mouth of the Mackenzie River in the Canadian Arctic, and from his observations reports:

	Year	
	1939	1940
Total nests	83	108
Total eggs	412	417
Average eggs per nest	4.96	3.8

Kortright (1942) states: "The black brant lays four to eight eggs but five seems to be the most common number."

Observations of workers along the Bering Sea coast have led to the conclusion that a clutch may average closer to four eggs. Broods are commonly reported as varying from one to five. As the season progresses, most observers find brood sizes diminishing.

One record of interest in Gabrielson's book (1959) concerns the data on seventeen nests located in the period June 19 to July 4, 1951, at

TABLE 3

NUMBER IN BROOD OF BLACK BRANT
Alaska Records

Number of Broods Observed	Average Number in Brood
34	2.26
159	2.01
31	1.71
224	2.01

Shishmaref—a district north of Nome—"with from 1 to 4 eggs." This indicates comparatively late nesting but also authenticates the small number of eggs in completed nests.

In 1949 Peter Scott and party visited the Perry River area of the Canadian Arctic. Here on a small island they noted the Pacific black brant as nesting birds in mid-July. In this area, which is probably near the eastern edge of the Pacific brant's nesting range, seventeen nests contained incubated eggs approximately five days from hatching. Most nests contained three eggs, one or two had only two, one was found with only one egg, and one with six.

In New Siberia, Pleske reports, eggs were laid the third week in June. He mentions that about the same time in 1902 Kolchak found these geese breeding at Kotelny Island; they had selected old gull nest sites and lined them with their own down. Three of the sets found by Kolchak contained but a single egg, and the fourth held three eggs. Late nesting is apparently the normal trend in this arctic frontier. On June 22, 1883, Dr. Bunge recorded finding the first nonincubated egg at the mouth of the Lena River, and on the day following, Sagastyr took a series of nests which contained, respectively, one, two, and three eggs. On July 12 in the same year, Koron found a nest at Cape Baranowski in which the five young were just hatched.

Danger of Egg Losses from Flooding

Reports of the studies conducted on the Yukon–Kuskokwim delta by U. S. Fish and Wildlife Service personnel in recent years do not carry evidence of nest losses by the black brant, but they do record disastrous storms and flooding in 1952. It must be presumed that over a period of several years flooding may again occur, causing losses on the sea edge, the favored nesting area of black brant. Records for 1963 indicate that a severe storm swept this area and there was little brood survival.

In 1937, at the height of the nesting season, the vast area along the islands of the lower Mackenzie Basin was flooded out; following the flood only a few pairs of black brant were seen attempting to carry on their renesting duties. But in 1938, reports Gillham, there was once again an abundance of birds, including the black brant, occupying areas which, only a year before, had been laid waste. Traditional nesting areas seem to have a persistent appeal.

Because brant nesting grounds must be low-level marshes affected by tidal waters on open bay shores, and because brant lay small clutches of eggs, rapid increases in black brant populations can hardly be anticipated. Gillham's report (1940) showed that on G Island, in the area of the lower Mackenzie River of Canada, three hundred nests in 1939 averaged 4.6 eggs per nest at the first nesting; and four hundred nests at the same location in 1940 averaged 5.6 eggs per nest. Second nestings due to flooding produced no eggs in 1939 and 3.15 eggs per clutch in 1940. Under the most adverse conditions, there might be very few young of the year surviving in the areas of catastrophe. Under the best conditions, the breeding pairs might show an increase of two hundred to three hundred per cent. The rapid upsurges that we have noted in such waterfowl as the pintails, widgeons, and mallards each time restraints were placed upon their harvest could probably never be anticipated if the brant were treated in the same way. Their small numbers, few breeding pairs, and lack of universal distribution make this obvious. A catastrophe such as a flood may affect a large segment of the species because of their communal nesting.

My observations in the nesting season of 1957 on the Kuskokwim–Yukon delta disclose that the reproduction of each pair could hardly be expected to increase brant flocks substantially, unless their life span was long and mortality of brant generally low, for the count of 161 broods averaged 2.51 young in late June. By the time they were airborne, the brood could be expected to show further decreases.

EARLY DAYS OF THE GOSLINGS

After the goose has incubated the eggs for from twenty-five to twenty-eight days, the young emerge and usually remain nest-bound for only a short time, about a day or less. They are more attractive than the goslings of the Canadas because they have a smoother symmetry and are more ducklike. In addition, they are more agile and the clumsy stumbling of the Canada gosling is not in evidence. They are sure-footed and follow their parents well. The dorsal coloration is uniformly a light charcoal gray in the first day of the gosling's life, and around each eye there is a light portion beginning at the top of the base of the bill and extending almost to the nape of the neck, as a straight line just below the eye, that sets off the beady eyes of the little brant, making them extremely attractive but hardly gooselike. This light color covers the neck and shades into the gray again on the breast, but the entire underbody partakes of the light grayish white. A light band crosses each little wing about where the primaries will later develop. By comparison, the Canadas have a body form which, even in their first days of life, makes them look somewhat malformed: they do not stand so erect, their breast bulges out to a noticeable degree, and the smooth, curved back of the adult goose is certainly not in evidence.

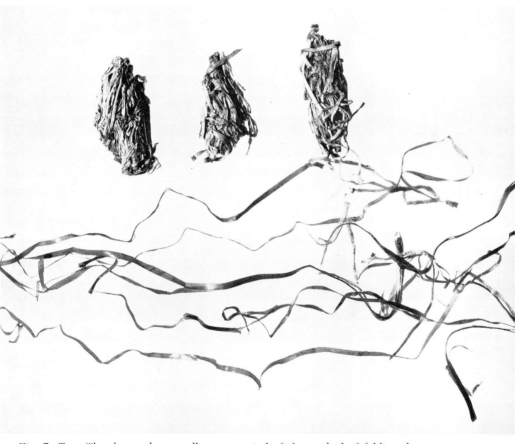

Fig. 7. *Top:* The three eelgrass pellets are typical of the method of folding that all brant use in eating this food. *Bottom:* Individual eelgrass fronds unfolded from pellets. (*Photo by author*)

Fig. 8. The number of broods produced in the summer habitat is few in comparison to the brant present. (*Photo by author*)

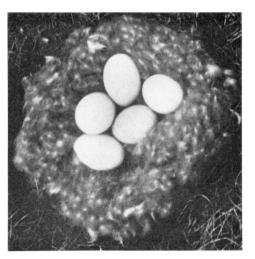

Fig. 9. The nest of the breeding brant is heavily lined with breast down. (*Photo by John Adair*)

Fig. 10. Access to the nesting grounds of the black brant is simplest by float plane. The plane was piloted by Axel Anuric, Eskimo pilot. (*Photo by John Adair*)

As soon as the goose leaves her nest with the goslings, the routine of development goes forward rapidly. Both parent geese are devoted to the care of the brood. There is little specific evidence of the varied items upon which the young goslings feed. It is obvious from watching them that they do take the tender parts of the sedge grasses, but there is probably a wide variety of choices, since they are active both on the land where insects abound and in the water where arthropods or crustacea and mollusks may be part of their diet; but this I cannot verify. They seem to have the puddling habits of ducklings, but this is one of the links in their life cycle that must be more thoroughly probed before a detailed and accurate list of foods can be isolated.

Since the midnight sun has come to the arctic tundra long before the goslings hatch, it is possible to find them active at any time during the twenty-four hours, and their day is a combination of intermittent feeding and resting with remarkably rapid growth as a result. When one is abroad in the murk at midnight, he may as often come upon a brood foraging on the tidal edge or the nearby marshlands as find them ensconced in the sedge grass being hovered over by the goose as the gander stands by.

The vigor of the goslings is surprising in birds so recently emerged from the egg. It would be a natural assumption that when first hatched they would be weak and would require a period of training so they could accustom themselves to the rigors of walking or swimming. Yet this seems to take no time at all, and the day after hatching the young will follow their parents either on land or in the water with surprising speed. Adult brant do not often dive, even in escape tactics, but the young will try to do so unsuccessfully in their first day of life, and they become adept in diving when only a few days old. After a week has elapsed, they are quite surefooted and will run rapidly, usually before the goose and the gander, and are not left behind unless the adults are pressed by intruders. Adults can run with surprising speed and even in their daily wanderings at the tidal edge will often run a mile down the shoreline and seem to be as much at home on land as in the air.

When pressed, they take wing and swing off rapidly, but if their goslings are in danger they do not fly away as the more timid birds do; they circle and call and soon the pair may be joined by other broodless birds and usually circle again and again in the intruders' close vicinity. It is doubtful if they ever desert their young under these circumstances.

The goslings are air-borne in about seven weeks. This is often the

height of the molting season, when the adults are flightless. The period
before the goslings reach self-sufficiency and the adults recover their
flight feathers is critical wherever Eskimo encampments are nearby.
Fortunately, this occurs in a very few places where the brant concentrations are at their greatest number. But when the combination does
occur, both the immature and adult birds become a part of the bag of
the natives. This is usually accomplished by drives of several natives
forcing the flightless birds into pre-erected nets. Where geese are not
numerous, the daily kill incidental to the usual activities on the tundra
may leave such an area unproductive.

6

Migration

There has always been something mysterious about the migration of waterfowl. There are none today, tomorrow they are legion. Where did they come from? How high did they fly? How long was their flight? Their appearance does not thrill the hunter alone: it is of interest to farmers or the white collar worker in the big city; it is noted in the press of the nation. A flight of geese or ducks in an unusual place, or under circumstances where they may be readily seen, brings headlines and reader interest if the situation is spectacular. Each of these wildlings has a pattern to follow, and in many ways these patterns are similar; but the black brant is a nonconformist and the sequence of events in its life on the nesting grounds diverges from that of other waterfowl.

On the tundra coast, where it clings closely to the seaward edge, its spring and summer habitat comprises a very small area. It is so restricted that for many years areas of heavy concentration lay undiscovered. When the young are air-borne, brant do not follow the practice of the other geese by drifting to feeding grounds in faraway places with the growing goslings. Nor are they like the pintail ducks, who start a drifting and wandering pathway in the sky to one marsh after another in early August, using a considerable area in daily flights that condition them for the long journey southward. The black brant clings quite tenaciously to its seaside home, and with the long arctic days the young grow rapidly and become fully fledged. This does not appreciably change the pattern of their home life, however. The sedge marshes like those at the mouth of the Yukon and the Kuskokwim hold them firmly in their grasp, until the shortening days of fall prepare the brant for another link in their life chain of events. This may occur in late August but usually falls in mid-September.

There are exceptions to this among the more mature nonbreeding birds because some of them begin to wander. In the records accumulated during this study, it was found that a few from such remote areas as the Canadian Arctic and Siberian coasts might be working down along the shores of the Gulf of Alaska in mid-August, apparently on their way south. They perhaps lacked the same urge of the breeding birds and their young, who still hold to the rearing grounds in late fall but eventually leave their northern home.

PREPARATION

It is not the first days of cold weather that stir them to leave the rearing ground. An early cold snap may be followed by a long spell of mild weather. Even in September they may not be forced by freezing from the marshes that have been their summer home. The urge comes to them, however, and with a little variation in timing the brant concentrate in vast flocks, coming down the coast in rapid flight and massive formation. One day on Izembek Bay there may be no brant, or at least so few that they almost elude the keen eyes and binoculars of an observer. The next day a flight of from twenty to thirty thousand may be observed winging swiftly in. All of them may come to rest in the bay to stay for a long time, usually several months. Then again this urge of migration, perhaps prompted by extreme cold, moves them, and they are gone until the following year. The returning birds and their progeny repeat the phenomena.

Izembek Bay, approximately thirty miles long, is located on the Bering Sea side of the Alaskan Peninsula. It is marginal to the ocean, but set apart by a series of barrier sandspits creating a much shallower waterway against the land. Outside Izembek is a series of sandbars, with gaps here and there through which the surging waters of Bering Sea wash in. The sandspits vary in width from a few feet to approximately half a mile. Some are covered with low vegetation but most are periodically awash—and the sands are sea-swept.

Robert Jones, currently manager of the Aleutian Refuge, familiar with the district and active on research for many seasons on Bering Sea and Bristol Bay, and Cal Reeve, a hunter and resident of the area, tell the same stories of the vast number of black brant surging in after a long fall period of almost total absence. The flocks linger long in their summer haven. But finally the day of travel arrives, the air is filled with their swiftly beating wings, and they come into Izembek.

In wave after wave, the brant fly into this unusual haven. Flocks may be so numerous that in some of the uncertain war days they caused an uneasiness in the minds of radar observers at nearby bases. The blips indicating air-borne objects covered the screen to such a degree that alerts were contemplated; but eventually the formation, while still afar, was properly identified.

When the brant arrive, they receive more than sustenance. The bay

offers protection from the storm because of its conformation and numerous islands. It is shallow and never becomes churned to the tempestuous levels of the deeper seas. Very few areas along the Pacific coast match this sanctuary. In many of their favorite bays, human activity combines the menace of hunting, the working of various boats, barges, and dredges, the continual shuffling back and forth of high-speed ships and small boats, and forces the black brant out into the ocean's surge. There, as we shall see, the hazards of life are great.

PATTERNS OF THE BRANT FLYWAY

Hochbaum's intriguing book, *The Travels and Traditions of Water-fowl* (1955), emphasizes clearly that pathways in the sky traditionally followed by waterfowl are evident to the observant person. To anyone familiar with the migratory habits of the black brant, this contention seems sound. Rarely do they approach over the land, although they may have courses that bring them near. On the Bering Sea coast they pass close to bold capes or headlands on the ocean's edge. At sandspits or sandheads exposed at low tide and extending into the sea, the brant may repeatedly skim by close at hand when searching for an emerging eelgrass bed, and if unmolested will pause on spits to loaf, preen, and obtain their grit.

At the present time the migration pattern of black brant is known to us only in general or partial outline. There is the general knowledge, for example, that when the breeding, nesting, growing, and conditioning season of the brant is well along in the north, there is a straggling flight southward from parts of the summering grounds, beginning as soon as late August. This flight appears to be made up of both immature and mature birds not of the year and unmated. There are occasional sight records of these migrations at a few points along the margins of the Gulf of Alaska and infrequent reports from boatmen such as the halibut fishermen working in the Gulf of Alaska, and on the ocean washing the southeastern Alaskan islands, and along the northwest coast of the United States.

There are few records of brant flying among the islands of the archipelago of the southeastern Alaska coast. J. Skog of Petersburg, Alaska, reported one brant taken on the inland waters at the mouth of the Stikine River near Wrangell, Alaska, in 1950. Another was reported taken in early fall of 1955 in Dry Straits at the head of Gastineau Channel near Juneau, Alaska.

The timing of the black brant's appearance, even at their favorite feeding grounds, varies greatly in the calendar year; but there is sufficient evidence of a flight pattern so that their arrival can be anticipated within certain periods. Concrete evidence of the early fall flights comes from Robert Welsh of Yakutat, Alaska, a pilot flying coastwise, who reports that in 1957 the first of the migrants passed through the Gulf of Alaska in the last days of August. In 1958 he first observed migrating brant in the second week of August. The first brant of the fall migration were not reported on the British Columbia, Washington, or Oregon coasts until much later. In fact, R. B. DeLong of Belfair, Washington, reported approximately one thousand black brant on October 28, 1957, in the upper Hood Canal area coming ashore to the sandspit almost in his dooryard, remaining but a few days, utilizing the habitat as a resting area, and then disappearing. By November 16, when the brant season opened, DeLong and A. Ottevaere of Bremerton found there were a few small flocks again using these waters. The indications are that these early arrivals come in to rest and then fly off, presumably to the Mexican coast, with the next arrivals coming directly from Alaskan waters and choosing the Puget Sound area for wintering.

Washington State is fortunate in having earlier arrivals of the species in a few places on the Puget Sound waters. Boundary, Samish, Dungeness, and Padilla bays often have a small population arriving in early or mid-November. After their arrival on Hood Canal in 1957, however, they were not seen in other spots on the Oregon and Washington coasts. A survey by the author in November indicated an almost complete absence of the species from such areas as the Strait of Juan de Fuca, Tillamook, and Netarts Bay of the Oregon coast. The report from Coos Bay from Robert Corthell, district game biologist, stated that even as late as mid-December only a handful of the birds were present in that feeding area, and none were recorded by William Breese on Yaquina Bay until after Christmas in that year.

From observations made in recent years, it appears that subsequent to the early flights to Puget Sound and Hood Canal in Washington, a small segment of the migration from Alaska comes directly to Puget Sound, occupying the traditional havens. At this time others may be noted on the ocean from Grays Harbor to Baja California. This is the greater part of the entire migration. Their goal is the wintering areas of Scammons and San Ignacio lagoons and Magdalena Bay in Mexico. This southern segment of the migration may include 40 to 70 per cent of the total black brant population. Information on their stay in Mexico will be presented in hunting data in a later section.

The largest concentrations of the brant do not appear in the Puget Sound and British Columbia waters until the northward migration from the havens of Mexico and California releases the wintering flocks. This time schedule varies, but the height of abundance occurs in late March and early April in the Sound area and the nearby British Columbia waters.

The sight records of Theed Pearse of Comox, B.C., kept over a forty-year period, outline the pattern of black brant arrivals and departures at several British Columbia localities on the eastern shores of the southerly end of Vancouver Island (Table 4). There are few records of abundance in this locale until after the first day of each year.

In the large concentrations of brant, particularly in the Puget Sound and British Columbia areas, where most birds are at the northern end of their annual migratory winter swing before returning to the nesting grounds, I have observed sudden fluctuations in populations. At such places as Dungeness Bay, Smith Island, Alki Point, Padilla and Birch bays, or other favored waters, there would be some morning in early April when I realized that what had yesterday been a host of brant, foraging among the eelgrass beds, was now drastically reduced.

We must conclude from the evidence that these birds flying along the migratory lanes toward the breeding grounds, reaching Alaska

TABLE 4

BLACK BRANT OCCUPANCY—FAVORED BRITISH COLUMBIA AREAS*

PLACE	EARLIEST ARRIVAL		SEASON'S PEAK		LATEST DEPARTURE	
	Date	No. Seen	Date	Highest No. Seen	Date	No. Seen
Elma Bay	11/11/34	4	4/25/48	2,000	6/2/48	14
Qualicum Bay	—	—	3/17/40	3,000	4/24/46	2,850
Kye Bay	—	—	3/17/40	3,000	5/1/46	170
Little River	12/14/32	Few	4/7/54	5,000	5/11/26	2
Seal Island	12/27/30	Few	4/13/36	1,000	4/15/56	80
Denman Spit	—	—	4/7/39	1,500	6/14/24	3 lots
Port Holmes	—	—	4/20/53	1,600	5/25/48	50+

* Theed Pearse notes, Comox, B.C.

areas like Dry Bay, Yakutat, the Kodiak Islands, and the Bering Sea areas in early April and May, are the mated pairs noted earlier in Baja California, the Pacific coastal states, and British Columbia. Because of their pathways of flight over the North Pacific, there are very few threads of evidence to indicate their exact route; but they are again noted in abundance as they approach their nesting grounds on the Bering Sea and the arctic coasts of Alaska and Siberia as far west as the Taimyr Peninsula. A day spent on some of the promontories is an enviable experience, limited to but a few naturalists. Those who have left good sight records are E. W. Nelson, Herbert Brandt, the U.S. Fish and Wildlife Service field personnel, and the more recent workers of the state of Alaska.

Concrete evidence of the North Pacific crossing was provided in 1958 by Terry O'Brien on one of the U.S. Fish and Wildlife Service exploratory vessels. He reported in correspondence with the author small flocks of brant on May 10 crossing the open ocean several hundred miles away from land in the Gulf of Alaska, where the closest landfall for the brant would have been the Kodiak Islands. He provided records on May 10, 11, and 12, and again on May 26. In each instance there were small flocks of approximately twenty birds flying at an elevation of less than twenty feet above the water. The usual speedy and determined flights were noted. From the knowledge of the departure dates from British Columbia and Puget Sound, it can be inferred that many of the late May observations must be of nonbreeding brant, since the schedule of nesting, incubating, and hatching would not permit these late arrivals to complete these duties successfully. The early arrivals on the tundra grounds, as reported by Robert Jones and other observers in or before mid-April and in early May, must be the producing segment of the birds, as broods are usually observed by early June. On the date of my visit to the Yukon-Kuskokwim delta about mid-June, 1957, most of the young were well developed. Obviously they had been hatched early in the month.

According to Pleske (1928), Baron Toll, reporting in 1904 from Bennet Island, the northernmost island of the group known as the New Siberian Islands, saw brant passing there in early summer. Where these brant were headed is anyone's guess. This treatise reports that in the New Siberian archipelago brant nest in very limited numbers only, but that later in the season they come in great numbers and molt there, selecting the outermost islands like Bennet and Wrangel. Further evidence is offered in a recent letter from John Adair, who noted brant passing Wainwright, Alaska, in late June, 1961; too late to be nesters, these birds were apparently seeking the molting areas of the Siberian coast.

In personal correspondence with Captain Joe Bernard, a friend of long standing and a naturalist famous for his association with the Siberian, Alaskan, and Canadian Arctic, working both as a trader and explorer, he has reported very little sign of large-scale brant nesting on the Siberian Arctic coast. His wide experience has convinced him that the segment of the brant population visiting Arctic Siberia consists mostly of unmated birds going there to molt. His observations accord with the records of Russian and European naturalists, whose data have been available in this search.

The annual orbit of the black brant covers a vast expanse. Their love for the sea and the low tide sea edges creates an image of geese different from the nostalgic, traditional impressions of geese in the sky. To the Eskimo, the Aleut, and the beachcomber, the undulating line on the ocean's horizon means a new season. The coming of the brant is eagerly awaited.

LIMITATIONS OF HABITAT

It must be remembered that the black brant have a very narrow choice of food and must seek out the waters where these forms abound. Eelgrass and sea lettuce are as vital to their survival as the air they breathe. Like the Florida coast limpkin, who search avidly for aquatic snails and leave the area if they cannot find them, the black brant are addicted to their diet. It is now presumed that the limpkin will eventually become extinct because the snails which sustain them are becoming scarce. Similar changes in the supply of eelgrass and sea lettuce, due to plant disease or the activities of man, may bring the black brant to extinction. In the early 1930's the scarcity of eelgrass, brought on by disease, almost caused the extinction of its eastern relative, the Atlantic brant. It took many years for them to begin to increase and former abundance has not been restored (Moffitt and Cottam, 1941).

As the black brant leave Alaska and work their way down toward the wintering areas of the Pacific coast, their flight usually terminates at some feeding ground or on the ocean nearby, from which daily flights can be made into bays and lagoons. Along the California coast, between Monterey and the Mexican border, there are few sheltered inlets, bays, and lagoons available to brant, for man has pre-empted this habitat. Storms are infrequent, however, and the coastal shelf is shallow—both invitations for the brant to feed and rest, at least for a short time, in the offshore kelp beds. On rare occasions they are even tempted to rest on the sandy ocean beaches, where they are temporarily unmolested.

But they do not come ashore for long; even when the hunting season is closed, the brant cannot use the beaches freely because beachcombers and skin divers are always there. The few inlets or lagoons they do use include Morro Bay, Newport Lagoon, Mission Bay, and the waterway and mooring basin off San Diego. Here, however, the human commotion sometimes proves too much. It is fortunate, then, that the open ocean is calm, for it is here the brant must usually go. The long coastal kelp beds offer food and a resting place without the surge of heavy swells or rollers. This makes the small feeding grounds vital to the black brant in this range.

In this area, too, brant have been seen coming ashore to spend the night. Observations of this habit were made near San Simeon along California State Highway 1 in April, 1956, where concentrations of ten to fifty brant were noted at several places. Here, in the dim light of the evening, they were seen on the sandy shores in the lee of boulders and rocks, islets, and promontories, just a few feet off the well-traveled highway.

In the better-known feeding areas of the Northwest, however, they make evening migrations to the open, safer waters, rather than coming into the shore. For example, flights from Padilla and Samish bays in Washington may be made each evening to the open waters of the Gulf of Georgia, where the brant drift for the night and from which they return to their feeding grounds the following morning. North of San Francisco there are few places along the coast where brant can be at ease and unmolested by natural elements. The surging surf washes the beach lines almost continuously, and it is rare, even in the late spring, to see them using the coastal eelgrass beds.

The inlets, then, are most inviting, and the brant are unerring, even at high tide, in dropping down to areas that will be useful to them when the waters ebb and expose their food. This has been observed innumerable times and only one experience need be related to verify this statement. Beginning in April, 1958, black brant were making periodic visit at the entrance to Alsea Bay near the town of Waldport, Oregon. For several weeks the brant were noted, in small numbers, at the bay entrance; but each time they were seen in only two limited areas, riding gracefully on the high tide and maneuvering to stay within certain limits as though they were held back by some barrier invisible to the human eye.

The reason for the choice of this spot, however, came into sharp focus when the beach was exposed at low tide, for there in two small triangles grew the food which obviously tolled the black brant into the area again and again. During the long period of their visits it was obvious that many different segments of migrants were using the same feeding grounds. Through tradition, perhaps, or the experience of the patriarchs or matriarchs in the flocks, awareness of the restricted feeding grounds persisted. It might also be that they do have a facility of vision for discerning feeding grounds even at the high tide stages. It is known that they can peer effectively into water and locate eelgrass at depths of several feet while swimming along, and their devotion to such small areas must mean that brant are dependent upon even these very limited resources.

Hunger is probably a persistent threat to a bird of such consuming energy. But brant are aware of their limited habitat and feeding restrictions, arriving at each haven as though it was a station listed on a schedule. Each year this routine is followed, though timing may vary slightly.

7

Hazards and Handicaps to Survival

Because brant do not nest in the shelter of a heavily vegetated habitat, they are menaced by both mammal and bird predators. The country is basically flat, and the terrain, with hummocks and mounds and chunks of driftwood scattered here and there, provides the predators with excellent lookout points. Because of early nesting, protective cover to shield the brant is lacking at these sites. Birds of prey on the wing can also survey a wide area, so brant face constant exposure to the feeding demands and hunting skill of their enemies.

MAMMAL PREDATORS

Throughout most of the brant nesting grounds, foxes are relatively abundant. There has been a drastic reduction in the number of foxes trapped in recent years, since the long-haired furs are not now popular in fashion, and there is little market. The white fox ranges along the arctic coast in considerable numbers, and as you move southward into the vast nesting ground of the Yukon–Kuskokwim delta, red and cross foxes are commonly seen. At the time of the year when they are having their pups and solid food must be brought to the den, they are an obvious menace to the nesting brant. As they press more diligently to pick up larger prey, ducks and geese are hunted to meet their family food quota until the pups can begin to hunt for themselves and may seek small rodents.

There are several signs that fox pressure is considerable on the brant nesting grounds. These include the presence of well-worn trails lead-

ing into the nesting ground areas where evidence of rodent populations may be absent. There are brant remains at favorite feeding spots
or at den entrances, and the continual wariness of the brant when a
fox approaches reflects their timidity. In our observations, the clamor-
ing of brant would often warn us of a fox's presence.

Present on the coast also are the mink, the weasel, and the wolverine. The mink of the Kuskokwim delta are large and dark in pelage.
Their food is based on availability; much of it is fish, although birds
are readily taken on the nesting grounds. Because mink are not gregarious and each family requires a considerable territory, their pressure on wildlife is not heavy.

With the smaller animal, the weasel, its lust to kill overshadows its
size. It will kill in a vicious orgy far more than it can possibly eat or
carry to its den. At Tacoma Prairie a few years ago, a pair of weasels
killed 157 two-week-old pheasants in a few moments. They, too, are
relatively scarce on the brant nesting areas, but a brood of young
brant would surely tempt the little killers, and brant were observed to
be alert to their presence.

The wolverine is a far-ranging predator with an omnivorous taste
for anything in the nature of food. No one can predict where this aggressive hunter of everything from man's supplies to mice may show
up. The awkward loping gait, its usual style of travel, will bring the
wolverine from the timber to the tidelands, although it is usually more
at home on the rolling tundra. In late September, 1958, in company
with Mike Utech and Cal Reeve, I saw a particularly large wolverine
cross the Cold Bay–Izembek road near the sea, miles from mountains
or timbered terrain. The animal saw us at a distance and loped to shelter, hiding in the hummocks. On this exposed tundra it was hunting
fearlessly in broad daylight, rather than awaiting the protective cover
of night. Food in any form is welcome, whether it be fish, fowl, or
beast, and nesting birds are particularly vulnerable. Its total pressure
on black brant, however, is probably less than on the wildlife of the
inland tundra.

In Gillham's field notes of 1941, he comments on the sled dog as a
waterfowl predator:

Untied dogs, abandoned dogs, and dogs purposely turned loose to avoid
having to feed them, are serious factors on waterfowl nesting grounds.

Dog feed is, and probably always will be, one of the most serious food
problems in the North. Practically all winter travel by the bulk of the popu-

lation is with dog teams. Airplanes, snow-mobiles and power transportation, while not always practical, are also very expensive. Dogs must eat, and sustaining food is preferably fish, seal, or white whale. Commercial preparations are not only too expensive, but the vitamin content and fat present is not sufficient for dogs to maintain health and do good work. Thus, dog feed, and large quantities of it, is the endless issue to be faced in the North. In spring months, when waterfowl nest, it is a temptation to turn the dogs loose and let them feed on waterfowl eggs, and later the young and moulting adults. This practice in the past was very common, though much has been done to discourage it.

It is the author's experience also that sled dogs will eat almost anything containing a flavor of food. One of the greatest hazards to their survival in the sled territory is the gulping down of the camp cloth dishrag which, by becoming impacted in the intestines without being digested, has killed many a valued animal.

But the day of the dog in Alaska is rapidly waning. The widespread air service in even the remote areas is astounding. There are dependable scheduled flights and, with adequate radio equipment at almost every public agency office, contacts permitting flight arrangements are made. Two-way radio sets at most business houses—even isolated stations—and in many homes make air transportation in Alaska almost a taxi business. The long treks with the dog teams are mostly colorful history, and Gillham's report of 1941 was probably written at the breaking point in tradition in the northland. His suggestion that air travel was costly seems to have little significance now. Even the Eskimo will not hesitate to pay fifty dollars to visit a neighboring village, then sit back in the cushions smoking his pipe in complete relaxation as though cost were nothing.

Another reason for the diminishing use of dogs is that trapping is no longer a full-time career for the Alaskan natives. The fox and wolf—predominant animals in the Eskimos' homeland—are both long haired, and their skins are not in demand. Because of the decrees of fashion and the prohibitive labor cost of precessing fur, only short-haired furs have been in moderate demand.

The long experience with dogs, however, has left the Eskimos with a fixation. In most camps, many dogs are still present but the full reliance on them for transportation does not exist. The menace to wildlife rests in the practice of allowing the dogs to forage for their food.

In the metropolitan centers, business and professional people keep the sled-dog tradition alive by keeping small kennels of racing stock, but they never see the nesting grounds of the waterfowl. Their foods are foreign to the land, probably consisting of the much-advertised mixtures that optimistically promise vigor, luster of pelt, or even chlorophylled breath, but which will never provide the same animal perfection that came from dried salmon, tomcod, or shee fish.

Only in a few places, where the Eskimos live in their primitive way in almost complete isolation, will the dogs search the tundra for eggs and birds. The prospect of severe inroads on the brant population by dogs is, therefore, remote. Successive generations of natives will sever their ties with the ways of the past and the colorful saga of the sled dog and his master will be ended.

BIRD PREDATORS

Many field observers find that birds of prey often select their nesting areas in close proximity to their source of food. Often they nest on the rookery of their favorite victims and swoop down on the harvest for their young.

On upper Ugashik Lake in June, 1922, I observed the predations of duck hawks on a local gull colony, taking each day as many of the young gulls as they needed to feed the hawklets. It has been noted by many that the black-backed and glaucous gulls often take up their nesting locations so that they can feed with ease on young shorebirds or waterfowl. This predator-prey relationship is particularly evident with waterfowl throughout Alaska.

Robert Smith of the U.S. Fish and Wildlife Service, a biologist who makes an annual survey of waterfowl breeding and wintering grounds, reports an instance at the mouth of the Anderson River in Arctic Canada, where he observed a glaucous gull swooping down to pick up a black brant gosling. It was immediately attacked by the gosling's parents who forced it to drop its prey, which then fluttered down and, in apparent good health, scurried for cover and protection. Shortly after this, in an unguarded moment, the gull again flew down and picked up the fledgling. This time it was forced to drop its prey by a sudden and severe attack by a single black brant. Smith's conclusion was that this little fellow was saved by the persistence, alertness, and aggressiveness of the adult black brant. It is to be noted that no other geese show either the aggressiveness or the aerial maneuverability to meet the marauding predators that may press the young, particularly in their early life. The black brant perhaps have an advantage over the other, more cumbersome geese in their ability to take wing rapidly without the combined efforts of feet and wings to put them aloft. A black brant may spring suddenly from the water or solid terrain, and, with its scimitarlike wings and swift beat, quickly overcome the lead of an adversary as ponderous in flight as the gulls.

Such a maneuver, however, would be pointless if the bird did not have the aggressiveness to force it into combat with a mammal or bird attempting to take a fledgling. That defensive capacity is not infallible can be recognized by the fact that survival of young in a brood hardly approximates 100 per cent. This is due to the long period that the parent geese must be alert, since the young are in continuous jeopardy for at least two months, and when the molt begins the adults lose some of their ability for combat. Their constant attention may be diverted for reasons of their own survival or even when they are occupied with normal activities; and in some instances their adversary may be clever enough to be successful and the best efforts of the parents are of no avail.

The jaegers are a continuous threat to eggs in the nest. On the brant nesting grounds of the Yukon–Kuskokwim delta, John Adair and I noted all three species—the pomarine, the long-tailed, and the parasitic jaegers—and saw nests and young of two species in June, 1957, near the habitat of the brant. These marine marauders are the hawks of the sea, powerfully built and showing a vigor and maneuverability when on the wing to compare with the masters of the air, the falcons. On the nesting grounds they were continually searching for fledglings they might steal. In my presence they even killed adult black turnstones in their aggressiveness to feed their young. Most of the observed jaeger nests were well inland from the Bering Sea edge. Those near the shelter cabin we occupied at Old Chevak were at least ten to twelve miles from the nesting grounds of the brant, but it was not unusual to see these predators winging home with prey for their young after a flight to the nesting concentrations of the shore birds and ducks along the sea edge. Like the falcons, they are swift fliers, and a ten-mile flight takes no more than a few minutes. Shore bird remains were common at the jaeger nests, but the evidence of depredations on eggs at the nests was observed only at the raided nest site. Carrying an egg for any distance would be difficult, although ravens and crows do this by selecting those of suitable sizes, such as shore bird and small duck eggs.

The fearlessness and vigor of the jaegers make them a continuous menace to black brant during nesting time and perhaps until the goslings are quite heavy. There are many records of egg loss, but newly hatched young probably fare better, since the breeding brant are more vigorous and alert to protect their goslings than are either geese or ducks.

C. E. Gillham, an observing naturalist and a regular visitor to the Canadian Arctic and Alaskan brant nesting grounds, wrote in his 1940 report:

The writer has, for six years, been constantly reminded by the natives of the North of the great destruction wrought by Jaegers in the nesting grounds upon the eggs and young of many birds, including Lesser Snow Geese. Recently considerable fear was expressed in Alaska of the destructive nature of these birds upon nesting grounds in that area. Control has been advocated of Jaegers in Alaska, and even in the Canadian Arctic, as a means of helping increase the continental supply of waterfowl and other birds.

The writer as far as he was able, made a complete study of Jaegers on the nesting ground of the Snow Geese and Black Brants. Eighteen specimens were taken at different times and stomach analyses later made of them by John Lynch in the laboratories of the Fish and Wildlife Service. These analyses isolated animal matter as their entire food demand.

From field analyses of these stomachs taken during the latter part of the nesting season, and from final analysis later made by the same stomachs in the U.S.A., the food habits of the Jaeger seem almost 100% bad. However, the following facts should be considered before the bird is entirely condemned, and possible control of this species recommended.

1. Geese this year scattered their eggs all over the nesting ground in un-

protected places, and left abandoned nests to the extent of 30% all over the area. These eggs were readily taken by the Jaegers and no doubt figured in the stomachs examined. However, it was noted that Jaegers preferred warm or incubating eggs, and utilized the abandoned nests in the main after the hatching season was completed.

2. Jaegers were greatly increased, 6 to 8 times as many, as last year on this area. This was believed to be due to the excess available food present, due to the abandoned nests and eggs present.

3. There was little evidence of Jaegers preying upon young newly hatched geese. It is felt that this bird is poorly equipped with the web feet for the taking of anything alive that can offer much resistance (but I noted a few instances of gosling kills).

4. . . . Jaegers broke up very few Black Brant nests. The brant is a fighter and more closely guards its nest. However, Eskimos from Banksland have told the writer of seeing several Jaegers combine in an attack upon a nesting brant and drive her from her nest, and then devour the eggs.

5. That Jaegers are feared by both geese and brants is manifest by the consternation shown by these nesting birds when their nest is closely approached by Jaegers.

A few times a group of Jaegers was observed flying and screaming about over an area where no nests of any kind were present. At first it was thought that the young of geese or brants were concealed in the grass, but this did not prove true. Some of the birds, usually but one, would alight on the ground and go flapping about in a most peculiar way. It was also thought that possibly these were courtship maneuvers of some sort.

Crane flies were observed, by Mr. Lynch, in some of the stomachs and it was his suggestion that the wing flapping demonstration had something to do with the catching of these insects.

The Eskimos are usually the most observant of any native people that I have ever met, but the ones of the Mackenzie Delta did not know of ever finding a Jaeger nest. On July 12 a pair of Jaegers near the Edward Hills were observed as remaining about one place on an open piece of tundra a great deal. Examination revealed the nest, laid on the moss without any concealment whatever, or any attempt at nest construction. It had two eggs.

On July 14, the writer returned to visit the nest. When a couple hundred yards from it, along a fringe of willows, the Jaegers flew screaming to meet him. At about the same time a pair of Willow ptarmigan and their 9 young flushed. One of the Jaegers immediately caught a young ptarmigan on the wing and flew away to devour him. An Eskimo assistant hastened after the bird and succeeded in retrieving the little ptarmigan, though he had been killed.

At the nest it was discovered that one young had been born (the other egg was infertile). The young was a dark steel gray, about the color of a very young black brant. The old ones screamed about, flying quite close to the Eskimo's head.

To take better pictures of the young and the old, the little baby Jaeger was moved to a distance of 12 feet from the writer and placed on a moss hummock. Almost immediately one of the adult birds swooped down, severely pecked the young bird, then picked it up and flew off with it. After flying about 200 yards it dropped the little bird, then alighted by it.

Again the Eskimo pursued the adult Jaeger, thinking this time the parent had simply rescued the young bird from us. He was surprised to find that the little bird had been killed.

Placing the young Jaeger back on the hummock, the adult bird twice again picked it up and flew away with it. The last time the Eskimo could not retrieve the little one and suggested that he thought the parent bird had devoured it. A few minutes later both birds returned to the nest where only the infertile egg remained. The writer shot both of them. Stomach examination proved that the parent bird had devoured his own young (it was the male bird) and had swallowed the little one whole with the exception of the head.

A third Jaeger now appeared and was also collected. He had been attracted by the screams of the parent birds, but was not one of the pair, as the writer had been working with only the pair and the little one for over an hour. The evidence was conclusive and positively proven that it was the male bird of the pair that devoured his own young.

The writer has little explanation for the above procedure, unless the Jaeger reasoned that the little one was to be lost anyway and he might as well eat it. The small bird was newly hatched, and it is more than possible that the parents do eat their young on occasion, or at least other Jaegers prey on their own specie. It is more than possible that such depredations might be responsible for the rarity of this bird, as they are not overly abundant. Certainly they should not be too numerous in the bird world, or other species would be endangered, and evidently they are not. It is to be remarked that any bird that would eat its own young, evidently would have small consideration for the young of any other birds that they might procure.

In addition to the pressure on their nesting grounds from birds of prey like the glaucous gull or the jaegers, the brant are faced with the harassing and predatory action of eagles whenever they approach the coast where these birds are either living or migrant. No eagles were noted on the Bering Sea coast during our visit to the nesting grounds of the brant in June and July, 1957, or at the premigration rallying area of Izembek Bay in September, 1958, although they are present in small numbers. But as soon as the brant reach the lower Pacific coast along the British Columbia, Washington, and Oregon shores, they find themselves periodically harassed by bald eagles. These birds are not selectors of certain species but are opportunists. Our records over a fifteen-year period at Protection and Eliza islands, Washington, revealed that most sea birds were vulnerable to their attacks; these included brant, cormorants, scoters, grebes, both puddle and diving ducks, and geese. Even the golden eagle exhibits the same aggressiveness. In company with L. F. Schneider near Alturas, California, in early April, 1955, we saw a golden eagle attack an adult Canada goose, turn it over on its back before it was dead, and begin to tear viciously at its breast, removing the skin and feathers from an area as large as a man's hand. When the eagle was frightened from the attack, the goose got up and hid in a tangle of cattails. There was no inclination on the part of the predator to return to its quarry during the time we were observing the situation. Because there were many geese in the vicinity, the eagle could strike down another goose at will, and this, perhaps, was its usual routine.

A former U.S. Fish and Wildlife Service game management agent, James Gerow, reported (1944) a brant kill on April 28, 1944, by a bald eagle diving into a flock of flying brant. It struck one down in a power dive from an 800-foot elevation, and the brant fell into Yaquina Bay. The eagle flew to the tide flats, waited a few moments, then retrieved the dead brant from the water. A pistol shot caused the eagle to drop its prey, which, when retrieved, showed deep and penetrating gashes in its back. During a one-hundred-mile flight along the British Columbia coast from Dodd Narrows to Campbell River on April 12, 1958, as a guest of Jack Beban, a black brant enthusiast, I noted six bald eagles resting in treetops. They apparently have little fear of airplanes, for two times we flew parallel with them approximately 300 feet above sea level, and they made no attempt to leave their perch, turning their heads to keep the plane in their range of vision. Obviously, we were not considered a menace.

With the black brant, however, the situation is entirely different. A plane flying even a mile or two away may cause either single or flocked brant to take to the air. They swing wildly into the air, in hurried and frantic flight, then, as soon as you overtake them, swing rapidly to the right or left in evasive tactics. This occurs even when the plane is in flight at heights of a thousand feet or more, which indicates that they are too wary to await the plane's arrival before taking off. This wariness has an adverse influence on aerial brant census flights, for they often take flight at great distances, and estimates or counts would be more easily obtained if they were less timid. Experience with birds of prey is perhaps the motivating force for their behavior.

Not all of the stoops on brant are successful. On January 21, 1959, on the edge of Tillamook Bay I collected an adult bird that was an escapee from such an attack. There was a gash on its body under its right wing and a claw mark of deep penetration in its right thigh. The brant was feeding on eelgrass drifting in as flotsam on the tide's edge; its wounds, uninfected and healing, clearly showed the typical spacing and abrasion of an eagle's attack.

The observations of most workers on the arctic and subarctic nesting grounds bear out the pattern of predator-prey relationship. Many wildlings survive at the cost of others in the chain of life decreed by nature. In the case of depredations on a species we personally cherish, we can become very bitter. I can hate with a great emotional stir the single great-horned owl that unerringly wiped out the colony of beautiful, big-eyed, soft, and harmless flying squirrels in my oak wood lot, or the bald eagle that killed a neighborly land otter which often dined on fish in our Eliza Island dooryard. But in the practical management of a species like the black brant, which finds in man the greatest hazard to an orderly and sufficient livelihood, the harvest of the jaegers, eagles, gulls, foxes, and dogs becomes merely a guide to hunting season limitations. Here is a concrete fact. If the brant of the year, produced by the breeding flocks—whose numbers vary greatly from one year to another—are but two per pair, then the harvest may be restricted. If production surges to the optimum level and perhaps five per brood enter the hunting harvest, or successive years bring relative abundance, greater liberalization should be considered.

There is a compelling thought to guide management harvests, however, when species are in continued short supply, owing to reproductive limitations, habitat restrictions, or scarcity induced by human actions. These three factors are critically evident in the lives of game birds like the prairie chicken, the sage grouse, the Wilson's snipe, and the black brant. The theory that liberalization in harvests results in more game has a limited degree of truth beyond which a thinking manager will not venture. Only live game can beget its kind, and it should be remembered that wildlife accounting is not relevant to the practices followed in money and banking. Good sense is the most essential requirement for the protection of individual wildlife accounts.

Predation, then, is but one of a series of conditions that must be recognized in management. The small toll, the price of one species preying on another, will probably never result in the extinction of a species, except when man has neglected to heed the species' obvious needs.

GROUND CRACKS

There is one natural handicap that may account for considerable losses of young goslings along the rivers, sloughs, and estuary banks of the delta area. Deep cracks in the soil are natural traps for goslings. This menace continues as long as the young geese cannot fly. Adult brant bring their goslings ashore at any point convenient to them. It may be at a place where the young find difficulty in following their parents. Most of the stream or slough banks are not sloping but abrupt. The entire nesting area is in a weather belt where severe cold locks the fresh water areas of the tundra in ice early in the fall. Eventually the sea also may be frozen to a depth of several feet.

Usually the arrival of spring comes earlier to the hinterland. In some years, the ice gorges pile up on the streams and when it begins to move toward the sea does so as a powerful gouging force. This mass of ice is forced against the banks when the river is at a low stage, or when the tide has reduced the sea level on the estuaries. These juggernauts undercut the banks like the blade of a powerful bulldozer. Some soil chunks are carried away but many rest on the bank edge. They are thrown together in a jumble with many interstices and caverns between the chunks. There are many cul-de-sacs for the trapping of the luckless goslings attempting to follow their parents.

While we were on the Kashunuk River estuary, we saw brant, emperor, and white-fronted geese attempting to bring their broods back and forth across this entrapping jumble of chunks. Each trip was a hazard. Here there were deep crevices perhaps a foot wide and several feet deep into which the goslings could tumble and from which the adults could not effect their rescue. Because the black brant usually select the lowlands marginal to the sea, and there is a continuous crossing back and forth from the tundra to the sea edge, this hazard can be a steady drain. The adults do not seem to select the hauling-out areas except as it meets their own ability, and the goslings, whether they be days or weeks old, naturally follow.

To determine how many goslings are lost in this way would be a difficult task, for one could not move the chunks of soil residue or know where to probe after the goslings had died. There also seems to be little chance of correcting such a condition. It is a natural hazard faced by brant, but must affect gosling survival and contribute to the decrease in brood sizes among the several species of geese nesting there.

The critical period when this situation may directly influence brood size is fortunately short. As soon as the young brant develop lifting power in their wings, this helps them to climb over the broken hummocks and may even help them out of a crevice.

HUMAN MOLESTATION ON FEEDING AREAS

After a survey of the entire area that is used as a wintering ground by the black brant, it is becoming more and more obvious that human molestation is one of the major obstacles to their survival. Black brant are extremely selective of their living range. As we have seen, two factors determine their choice: the presence of eelgrass, *Zostera marina*, and sea lettuce, *Ulva* sp., which make up the bulk of their food; and suitable grounds where they can loaf, preen, and acquire the gravel they constantly need. There also seems to be an occasional need for fresh water, although brant often drink sea water. Each spring in Kilisut Harbor, Marrowstone Island, Washington, brant regularly drink from a beachside spring seep of fresh water. At beachside creek outlets near Dungeness, Washington, brant congregate each spring to enjoy the fresh water.

Eelgrass beds suitable as feeding areas must be exposed at some stage of the tide, since these birds do not dive. Where the tidal range is limited, as at Izembek Bay, food is more readily accessible. In areas of extreme tidal ranges, the food is exposed for shorter periods, and during severe storms it may be continually covered. In this situation free-floating remnants may be all the brant can glean, and this limits the amount of foraging area the birds have. Abundant eelgrass growing too deep to be exposed contributes very little to the daily food demands of the birds and is thus not a dependable source of supply. It consists of the fronds that are broken off seasonally or from mechanical action during heavy seas, but it does not amount to enough to supply the daily wants of the birds. In the winter months, when low tides are usually at night, the brant attempt to feed all day long, searching the surface of the waters aggressively to gather what is available. The fact that they are persistently active indicates that their hunger is never quite satisfied. Neither ducks nor other geese face the same problem, since they can choose from a wide variety of foods readily available and palatable to them.

Three situations seriously influence the feeding of the black brant:

1. The lack of exposed eelgrass beds is often critical on wintering waters. Availability is limited by storms, which prevent normal runouts of the tide, and the feeding day of the brant is much restricted by darkness. Most of the extremely low tides of winter fall during the periods of darkness, when the birds are naturally handicapped.

2. In some areas, boating activity continually molests birds seeking food in their usual places. During the last five years the high-speed boats, especially with outboard motors, have become so numerous that they are found to course almost continuously on many favored brant feeding grounds, which makes the areas untenable to the species. This is a common practice from British Columbia to San Quentin Bay in northern Baja California.

3. The use of mechanical equipment, particularly power dredges, intimidates the feeding birds in daylight and tends to destroy the favored eelgrass beds. These should be protected. Where possible selected areas should be set aside in strategic places for wildfowl. Oystermen use gravel or shell to make the beds firm, which often excludes growing marine plants, the food of survival for the brant.

In Morro Bay, California—a traditional winter habitat that has maintained several thousand birds at a time in the past—the flocks of black brant are decreasing each year, since they are continually disturbed by the power dredges that have destroyed portions of the eelgrass beds. In company with L. F. Schneider on January 18, 1958, I observed brant trying persistently to enter Morro Bay to feed. A small area approximately three miles long and a mile wide encompasses the territory that might be useful to the brant if they are left there unmolested. But a large portion of this area is now occupied by oyster beds. During our visit, oyster dredges were constantly working back and forth, intimidating the birds who had come in to feed. There was a continual shuffle from the open ocean to the bay, for the disturbing conditions never ceased and the brant were forced to return to the ocean after each reconnaissance flight. Unfortunately there is no adequate sanctuary maintained in this bay for brant.

Oyster farming in bay areas is a practical and needed activity, but since much of the bay areas is state, federal, or county owned, the reservation of favored waterfowl habitats is as much a part of good government as other segments of public operations.

In areas of sudden surges in human population, and in stable communities as well, people turn to any diverting outlet to use up idle time. Conservationists have been and will be cursed with the onus of preventing excesses against nature. A staff of public employees geared for a stable population may find a sudden population increase that may double the number of recreation seekers. Morro Bay is such a place. Much of the vandalism we face today as the result of more idleness could be abruptly curbed by citizens' intervention and relaying facts to the enforcement officers. The public generally lacks the realization of what is a thrifty use of our wildlife resources. Such training should begin in the home and continue in every grade of our public schools. In this we are seriously lacking.

Better management and habitat adjustments to permit the wildfowl to utilize fully at least a part of their traditional feeding ground are imperative. The following experiences of the late J. A. Munro (1957) offer a good example of this need:

In studying the background of a waterfowl population which has been subject to man's influence over a long period it is desirable to consider not only the part man has played in re-shaping the environment but to consider also the current man-bird relationship. It is, regrettably, a fact that pleasure in shooting harmless wildlife for no other purpose than that of actual killing is a common enough human activity, restricted to no particular geographical area. At Morro Bay, however, the sport, if it may be called such, has reached proportions unparalleled elsewhere in my experience. Here the custom of using water birds as targets for shotgun and rifle practice is carried on during the hunting season continually, conspicuously, and increasingly as the passing years bring greater numbers of hunters. Evidence supporting this statement is the fact that after every weekend shoot there is an accumulation of dead birds along the bay shore that through the season contains examples of all species of waterfowl which visit the bay, ranging in size from least sandpiper to white pelican.

Thus on January 29, 1954, a total of 89 dead birds was counted on approximately one mile of the west shore of the bay, the species and numbers of each being: common loon 1, arctic loon 1, red-throated loon 8, black-necked grebe 4, western grebe 3, double-crested cormorant 2, Brandt cormorant 1, black brant 13, pintail 8, shoveller 2, baldpate 5, lesser scaup duck 2, white-winged scoter 1, surf scoter 8, black-bellied plover 1, willet 10, red-backed sandpiper 1, marbled godwit 7, red phalarope 1, glaucous-winged gull 4, western gull 1, herring gull 1, royal tern 1. . . .

During the 1956–57 hunting season, from November 7 to February 10, I examined a total of 506 dead birds, the majority of which had drifted on to the section of bay shore referred to above. The number was made up as follows:

Common Loon	5	Dunlin	3
Arctic Loon	4	Long-billed Dowitcher	1
Red-throated Loon	9	Western Sandpiper	32
Horned Grebe	19	Marbled Godwit	20
Black-necked Grebe	34	Sanderling	5
Western Grebe	65	Avocet	3
Pied-billed Grebe	8	Glaucous-winged	12
White Pelican	14	*Black Brant*	98
Brown Pelican	2	Pintail	6
Double-crested Cormorant	13	Baldpate	7
Brandt Cormorant	3	Shoveller	2
Pelagic Cormorant	4	Green-winged Teal	7
Great Blue Heron	1	Buffle-head	1
Snowy Egret	1	Surf Scoter	2
Whistling Swan	1	Ruddy Duck	21
American Merganser	1	Western Gull	12
Red-breasted Merganser	3	Herring Gull	4
American Coot	34	California Gull	2
Black-bellied Plover	2	Ring-billed Gull	7
Long-billed Curlew	3	Heermann Gull	1
Willet	25	Royal Tern	1
Knot	1	Foerster Tern	3
Least Sandpiper	3	Kingfisher	1

The totals of non-game birds shot undoubtedly exceeded those in the above enumerations, one reason being that only a part of the shoreline came under observation; furthermore no attempt was made to search through the windrows of eelgrass and debris which could have concealed other bodies.

One of my objects in visiting Morro Bay was to collect a series of waterfowl. In achieving this purpose I soon found that a gun was rarely necessary, and more often than not no gun was carried. Indeed the supply of dead birds frequently was so large that, lacking refrigeration storage, only a small portion of those available could be prepared.

Stuart L. Murrell, a good observer, reported seeing only one brant during a week of observation in the 1958 Christmas season at Morro Bay; and in early January, 1959, only three black brant were seen by the author on this bay.

Another boating disturbance—though this was perhaps less dramatic than the episode on Morro Bay—was observed on Mission Bay, which is part of San Diego Harbor, on January 19, 1958. Here at low tide the black brant could find sanctuary only in the small elbows off the main channel in the bay, where they could drift up a mud-bottomed slough for perhaps a few hundred yards; but the continual rushing back and

forth of high-speed inboard and outboard boats, which traveled at ve-
locities of from eight to forty miles per hour, prohibited the birds from
foraging on eelgrass beds or occupying the open water in the channel.
A surging stream of recreationists was moving back and forth, and
brant were continually in the air, seeking some escape from the speed-
ing boats and searching in vain for a single place where they could
feed normally. The increasing number of boats of all kinds, the speed
at which the craft move, the indifference of the operators, and, to some
degree, the aggressive lawlessness of those who ignore all regulations
and simple standards of ethics are a menace to brant survival.

Boating activity on Humboldt Bay, California, is also forcing brant
to spend their nights on the ocean. Serious losses are occurring, for in
the hours of darkness sleeping brant drift unconsciously into the
breakers where the heavy sand content of the breaking seas beats
them down to the ocean floor and they wash ashore as "sanded" dead.
Many are found along the ocean beaches, although their number does
not reach that of the larger flocks of ducks. Of the latter, the state and
federal wardens retrieved 479 in one day on the ocean beaches off
Humboldt Bay in December, 1958. Their report from the Office of the
Regional Director of the U.S. Fish and Wildlife Service follows:

> A total of 479 dead ducks were picked up along the beach at South Spit
> near Eureka, California. The birds apparently had been sanded during the
> night. Occasionally waterfowl resting on the water just outside the breakers
> will drift into them. The breakers roll the ducks under with sufficient force
> to kill them. Most of the ducks killed were widgeon excepting six pintail and
> two teal. Birds were delivered to the Humboldt County Prison for its use.

Molestation by man is an increasing hazard to the brant along the
entire coastline visited by these migrants. Their plight emphasizes the
need for properly spaced refuge areas which are largely lacking.

COMPETITION WITH MAN'S NEEDS

A recurring irritation to the fishing public are the diving ducks,
grebes, brant, and other waterfowl which move in to feed when herring spawn collects on eelgrass beds. In Puget Sound, Washington,
early in 1958, sportsmen, instead of recognizing that sea birds must
feed, brought pressure upon game management agencies to remove
the birds from the herring spawning areas by any means. The matter
was given considerable publicity by the sports-writing fraternity, as
though Angler Club edicts could render divine powers to game de-

partments to change the habits of both fishes and birds; or perhaps it was thought that the birds should be sacrificed to insure a fancied human right.

Those responsible for management have usually taken the position that there is a chain of life in the waters which, when broken, brings on crises of serious proportions. The herring are a link in the chain of survival of many fishes and other wildlife. Since in this area it is in precarious supply generally, it must be kept in fine balance with the habitat and its uses. In many years it has been deemed best to draw upon the "runs" only sparingly, but even with this approach there have been several periods of serious exploitation. For many years herring in the state of Washington had been supported by regulations that restricted their use to "food or bait." This was a wise conservation proviso. The demands for these purposes have generally been modest and no serious drain upon the fishery.

In the early thirties, management personnel saw fit to liberalize the taking of herring and pilchards, permitting them to be made into oil and fertilizer, a manure for the soil. The business venture failed in a few years because the supply dwindled to general scarcity. To use whole food fish of quality for fertilizer is wasteful. In 1958 a harvesting liberalization was again put into effect, and the herring were again exposed to decimation. The fish were scarce. The take, however, may have had retarding effects on many species of wildlife. To perpetuate the brant, management of herring and other limiting influences may be a part of a survival program in the future.

8

The Brant as a Game Bird

Black brant are a prized species for the understanding waterfowl hunter. To the true wildfowler or naturalist, wonderful days in the habitat of the bird are as much a part of the "harvest" as the uniformly high quality of the bird when it is properly prepared for the table. Obviously, the brant will never be in great abundance. Other forms elsewhere in the world have similar values because habitat limitations hold them in check. Well-disciplined harvests are the only way to sustain minority species. In the Scandinavian countries, the crawfish is living on the margin of its habitat, as is the Atlantic salmon. Yet for many years they have been sustained at stable levels by a careful attention to management, and the annual harvest, though it may last but a few days, is a time of festivity and enthusiasm. This is a better philosophy than the usual "heavy feast or famine" attitude. It will engender a much more thrifty attitude toward all our natural resources. It will bring stability to those forms adaptable only to limited ecological niches. To hasten their end by an indifference to their needs, and to presume that abundance in the hunter's bag is the lone criterion of success, can only lead to barren habitats everywhere.

In any community where the birds may be taken, you will find dedicated hunters. This clan is small, though persistent. The surroundings associated with the sport, the various skills that must be mastered, and the elusive emotional urge that makes one a brant hunter rather than a devotee of general waterfowl shooting all combine to reduce the potential harvest. If it were not for these deterrents, the black brant would now be scarce or absent. They have been available since the first settlers reached the Pacific coast, but in relatively small numbers. Early explorers and pioneers rarely reported these geese in abundance, hence management today must deal with a species that has a small margin for exploitation.

Nowhere is there evidence that brant have suffered the gun pressure comparable to that pressed upon the canvasbacks, redheads, or other ducks. If such had been the case in the days when good guns and ample ammunition first became available, the black brant would now probably be a bird so reduced in numbers that their restoration to levels of harvest would be a venture of doubtful outcome.

Migratory and Seasonal Range

As the birds move southward from summering ranges, their late arrival determines the period of open hunting season. Usually this is not until late November or early December in British Columbia or the Pacific coastal states. Often only a few straggling skeins of brant are found on their traditional havens then. As the year wanes, the numbers increase because of birds drifting back from Mexican waters, the destination of most of the fall flights.

Alaska

There is a wide stretch of territory in Alaska where the black brant may be hunted. Hunting starts in a limited degree east of Point Barrow and passes the Point; then there are a few strategic spots along the entire Bering Sea coast reaching to the Aleutian chain. The inlets and lagoons near False Pass mark the southern limit of the best hunting areas. There are some key concentration points where the migrant brant pass in large numbers and where they could be readily taken by gunners if the area were heavily populated.

In the northland the groups that seek out the black brant with greatest persistence are the natives: the Eskimo and the Aleut. These people are continually searching for food, and the eggs, the young, and the adults of the brant are all used. Late fall ushers in colder weather conditions, which permit them to keep and successfully store food. The period of abundance is short. At a few strategic locations, where the brant fly past a sandspit or headland, the natives take their modest harvest. By Hansen's estimate, the take of brant is only 10 per cent of the goose total, with Canadian geese making up the greatest part of the kill.

The Eskimos of the Alaskan tundra who live in the Yukon–Kuskokwim delta occupy a strip approximately 250 miles long and 150 miles wide. This is the basic nesting ground of the brant. On the seaward edge, the flow of the tides may cover vast strips of marginal land, and with the periodic storms, when tides rise five or six feet above normal, the surge of the sea sweeps inland many miles, reducing the total land acreage by almost a third. Throughout this vast alluvial fan the amount of high ground is almost infinitesimal, and there are not many islands of safety or suitable permanent home sites. Most of the seasonal home sites of the Eskimos, their base for summer activities, are endangered by the occasionally extreme tides or the run-off floods caused by ice gorges in the rivers and streams during the spring months. Even at Bethel, which is normally considered a protected location, floods on the Kuskokwim River have periodically caused serious damage.

The entire tundra area between the Yukon and the Kuskokwim rivers is approximately 40 per cent water and 60 per cent land; a land of endless pools and lakes. Because of the proximity of the land to sea level, the Eskimos' use of fishing and hunting camps is limited. They may return season after season to a favored spot, but it must be at times when conditions will permit this, since year-round living is not possible at most of these locations. The Eskimos have long been a wandering race, very dependent on nature for their sustenance. During the summer months they live in tents, following the wildlife as favorable opportunities occur. They usually prepare for the severe winter weather on higher ground: in sod houses known as *barabaras* if they have chosen to spend the winter at the outposts; or in board houses of rather poor structure if they have joined some of the permanent colonies, particularly during the school season.

The best estimates that can be procured on the shifting Eskimo population in an area so vast and in such a remote section of Alaska indicate that approximately fifteen hundred natives occupy the tundra between the Kuskokwim and the Yukon rivers in the area suited for waterfowl breeding. If this area were allotted in equal units, each Eskimo would have approximately sixteen thousand acres—or five square miles—upon which to range. It should be mentioned that this tundra is considered the most densely populated Eskimo habitat in Alaska, although a few concentrations of Eskimos are almost metropol-

Fig. 11. The stool of decoys are out. They are moved periodically as the tide recedes. (*Photo by author*)

Fig. 12. Scull- or sneak-boats are still in use to outwit brant. (*Photo by author*)

Fig. 13. Offshore stilt blind in South Humboldt Bay. (*Photo by George Black and Charles Chambers, U.S. Fish and Wildlife Service*)

Fig. 14. A shoreside blind, Humboldt Bay, California. (*Photo by George Black and Charles Chambers, U.S. Fish and Wildlife Service*)

itan in aspect, as at Point Barrow. During the waterfowl breeding season, the Eskimos may be distributed over much of the nesting ground. They will be found in small groups, rarely exceeding twenty, of all age classes. Each camp is situated at some strategic location so that transportation by water is an aid in harvesting the natural food of the area.

The life of the Eskimo, as a nomad on the arctic and subarctic shores, bears no resemblance to that of anyone in our cosmopolitan world. Unlike the Eskimo, the average man we know does not struggle endlessly for self-preservation. He probably aims his entire existence at physical and mental comfort. He is concerned most of all with his own happiness. As a result, the life pattern that periodically crushes

Harold Cramer Smith

civilized people usually has no relation to the basic needs of survival. With the Eskimos this is never true. Before them lie the daily needs of sustenance. In many instances a family or an entire village may have no food for tomorrow.

When we were in the tundra, we camped in the little community church of Old Chevak and from the surrounding evidence of camp sites, the decaying barabaras, and other remains, we could presume that approximately ten to fifteen families had occupied the site before removal to the New Chevak center about ten miles to the northwest. There were signs, too, that the colony had remained nearby for several generations at least. Well-worn camp discards offered mute evidence of the passing time.

The small solitary cemetery on the highest ground to the southeast of the camp contained sixty-eight graves—about half adults and half children. The cherished articles of the dead left to help them in their spirit world indicated that they were from all levels of Eskimo society.

Graves of the chiefs were obvious, as were those of the more lowly. Even the treatment of the children's graves indicated both poverty and comparative wealth. Their wants were long gone; and the wily ptarmigan, the grouse of the tundra whose race has contributed consistently to the subsistence of the Eskimos of that area, outlived the hunters and now nested in the cemetery. Each morning the cock birds would mount the high cross on the chief's grave and challenge their neighbors, or in the hours of midnight come to the window of the old church and disturb our slumber with scolding calls. In the predawn gloom of the longest days of the year, they could be heard as they assessed the nature of an intruder, usually a red fox.

The hazards of life, the ravages of malnutrition, and the missing immunity to the diseases of the white man have always spelled a precarious and foreboding career for the Eskimos of the tundra. Today the Eskimos are handicapped further by inclinations produced by watching the white men. As a result, they have cultivated habits and desires out of keeping with their normal way of life. This is aggravated by closer contact with modern commercial outlets whose motives of profit weaken the communal life of the Eskimos.

The craving for honor, recognition, and respect among them is as keen as that in other peoples. Traditionally, it has been engendered by the ambition, the skill, the patience, and persistence of a hunter who by his productiveness has become greatly respected. By these attributes, he could pull himself above the level of the ordinary person in the village. His contributions of food kept the specter of starvation from many igloos.

We in our modern world have no conception of the patience, perseverance, and hardship suffered by the Eskimo in his habitat. It has made his race a people apart. The reason they call their kind the Innuit, the "man people," is to identify themselves as distinct from the spirit people or animals. The description fits. They are truly of real stature in coping with nature. Admittedly, they are wasteful of food when it is abundant, which may be justified as simple satisfaction after experiences of food scarcity. With their hunting tools, however, they are never wasteful when living as primitive man; the care they show in guarding them contrasts markedly with the waste and carelessness we show toward our own beautiful tools. In many instances, a whale spear will serve its maker throughout his entire life, and it may eventually appear as one of his most cherished possessions on his grave. It

is astounding to see the time-worn implements in a collection of arti-
facts and equipment of the natives of this range. They have been in
daily use for perhaps fifty or sixty years, and have become known and
respected as the talisman of an individual. If found after having been
lost, they are returned to the owner, simply because they are recognized as surely as if the man's name were written upon them. Thumb-
prints on an FBI identification card could be no more revealing.

Whether he hunts for self-preservation or to obtain items for barter,
the Eskimo must follow the dictates of nature; and the shrewder he is
in the lore of the wild, the greater the benefits. The simple problem of
food scarcity has trained him to show a never-failing interest in the
natural resources of his land and a canny skill in harvesting wildlife.
He even decoys some species by making facsimiles or by simulating
their action.

Though it may often be meager, the most consistent food supply
comes from the marine waters. The land forms in the cold and un-
yielding soil of the northland have surges of scarcity and abundance
that would make it precarious for any race to depend entirely upon
this source. It is imperative, then, that the Eskimos be opportunists. In
this enlightened age, when we as citizens of the North American continent pay subsidies for food we do not need, it is hard for us to understand that the Eskimos may work persistently for days in catching tiny
sticklebacks, two inches long, in order to eat even frugally. This fish
must be taken in a quantity that only persistence, patience, and vigorous effort can produce in order to supply enough to fill a single person's wants. By our standards, any food in such short supply would be
completely ignored, but with that viewpoint the Eskimos would surely
perish. Hence it is that with each surge of wildlife population the Eskimos are at hand to utilize it as fully as possible. When the migrant
waterfowl, fish, or sea mammals are anticipated, there is a shift to the
favored rallying points.

We are inclined to believe that with our refuge system we are providing the waterfowl who enter the United States from the northern
nesting grounds with a substantial portion of their needs. We would
be quickly impressed with the restricted range that we have allotted
these birds if we were to visit northern Alaska or Canada and see the
vast stretches of territory necessary to supply the minimum requirements of even such gregarious birds as the black brant.

In conversation with many enlightened people whose principal recreation is hunting, I have found erroneous conceptions of the nesting habits of our waterfowl. Generally, it is presumed that the birds are very gregarious and join together in what might be loosely termed a "colony" or "rookery," and with the vast territory available in the northlands, there is no scarcity of opportunity for the nesting birds to bring off a full complement of young each year. With this viewpoint it is hard to understand that each nesting pair claims a habitat that may be miles from its neighbor.

This is not true of the black brant, for they will nest close to each other. The white-fronted geese may follow a similar inclination. But most of the nesting pairs demand much more range than we seem to visualize in our casual references to a well-stocked nesting ground. For that reason, then, the Eskimos do not find the tundra a complete utopia in harvesting eggs, young, and adults, all of which would help them in their daily food wants. There is only one time in the year when an abundant harvest is possible in the land of the Eskimo, and that is during the flightless stage of the adults during molting time. Then both young and old can be surrounded and driven into sizable bands for the kill. But this period, when the birds are most vulnerable, is relatively short. It is at its peak for perhaps eight or ten days, and lasts no more than fifteen days.

During this time the black brant can be easily taken, since they can be surrounded either on the tundra or on the water and forced into nets for capture. However, the black brant favor selected margins of the sea fronts and this location, far from the usual fishing camps, is inconvenient for the Eskimo, for this is the time of year when his main sustenance is fish—which remain available for long periods of time—and the days he must devote to hunting black brant represent a seasonal opportunity only.

A processed paper, "Utilization of Wildlife by Alaska Natives," prepared in 1957 by Henry A. Hansen, biologist of the U.S. Fish and Wildlife Service, and supervisor of the Waterfowl Investigations, contains some estimates of waterfowl and eggs taken by Eskimos. The following paragraphs on the nesting and shooting seasons are revealing:

On a per capita basis, the Barrow Eskimos took 7.7 ducks per individual according to Remington's account and 2.9 ducks per individual by their own tally. By way of comparison, the Kotzebue Eskimos reported taking 10,000 ducks (11.5 per capita for 869 individuals). A further comparison is possible on the lower Yukon where River Basins biologists spent two summers on a fisheries survey. Toward the end of this period, after they had gained the confidence of most of the Eskimos, the biologists conducted the game utilization survey within some of the villages (in which) they had been working and living. In four of the villages totaling 530 people, the survey was considered to be quite accurate. These people admitted to 1,715 ducks (3.2 per capita) and 3,830 geese (7.2 per capita) compared with an average for the remaining 13 villages (1,569 people) on the Yukon-Kuskokwim delta of 4.6 ducks per capita and 3.7 geese. Waterfowl abundance and hunting opportunities should have been quite comparable throughout this homogeneous unit on the lower Yukon. The most surprising difference between the four selected villages and the remaining 13, however, was in the reported harvest of swan and crane. The four villages reported taking 507 swan and 474 crane whereas the other 13 villages reported only six swan and 70 crane. The distribution of swan and crane should have made them almost as accessible to any one of the 17 villages as to another. From the biases and inaccuracies noted above, it is evident that the utilization figures would not withstand a statistical scrutiny, but it does appear, however, that the total migratory bird figures, at least, indicate a very substantial annual harvest and might even be accepted as minimal.

During the interview among the Natives, an attempt was made to determine the percentage of non-game ducks versus game ducks. Non-game ducks refer to scoters, eiders and old squaws which would not enter the Stateside kill under any circumstances. Frequently all the ducks were listed together but of those separated on the questionnaires 78 per cent were listed in the non-game category. Except for brant, no game species were listed among the waterfowl harvested at Barrow. Many of the questionnaires on which all ducks were unclassified indicated in an explanatory sentence that most of the ducks taken were scoters and old squaws. Other reports from the field indicate that the sea ducks are taken by Eskimos and Indians by preference. They prefer both the larger size and the stronger flavor. Preference for large sized birds, and the greater ease with which geese are captured during their flightless period, is also indicated by the high percentage of geese in the over-all kill, one-third of the total. Roughly, one-half of the geese are sub-species of Canada goose, about 35 per cent are white fronted geese, about 10 per cent are black brant and the remaining five per cent are snow and emperor geese.

Of course, availability takes precedence over preference in the utilization of game in various areas. Also, the extent of hunting and trapping effort is tempered by the amount of wage labor and various sources of relief accruing to individual villages. Wildlife utilization fluctuates in somewhat of an inverse ratio to the size of the annual cash crop with which to buy the necessities.

The gathering and utilization of eggs is common in all villages where nesting birds are available. Biologists working in some of the Yukon Delta villages have observed that the eggs of any species from robin-size on up are gathered diligently by women and children and that the aggregate take for some villages must be relatively great. This is particularly true near the coast where colonial nesting species are available. Of the 58 villages sampled, a total annual take of 10,700 eggs was reported. The majority of these eggs were collected from colonies of gulls, murres, puffins and other sea birds. Thus, an expansion of eggs utilization from coastal villages to interior villages would be extremely biased on the high side unless a correction factor were used and there is none at hand.

Since there are so few Eskimos living in such a vast territory, it is probably impossible for them to hunt and destroy the nesting birds on the breeding grounds. That they will continue to harvest available food from nature must be the acceptable pattern, and restraints that can easily be placed upon them should be well considered. In fact, interference in their frugal way of life should be one of the last steps taken, for these people occupy an important niche in our country. By living on a marginal frontier that is difficult for either our civilian or military personnel to occupy successfully, the Eskimos can be invaluable in our defense programs. They can fill the serious gaps in our knowledge of that vast hinterland.

Other sources of human influence in this range might eventually develop. The nearest city of size that might bring pressure to bear on the migrating geese is Anchorage. It is a busy city. In the last twenty years it has passed from a village to a modern metropolis, with a population surging seasonally from fifty-five thousand in its immediate environs. Most of its people are conditioned for life in this vast hinterland. Evidence of this is found in the quick restoration in the earthquake-damaged city and the loyalty of the residents to their community.

It is significant that the metropolitan population, which is predominantly interested in less arduous recreation and spectator participation, makes up only a small percentage of the total population. The male population as a whole is concerned with the outdoors as indicated by a brisk market in sporting goods. The ratio between rifle and shotgun sales is about twenty to one, which is approximately the relationship between the big game and the waterfowl hunters.

Because of the limited number of birds found on the mountain slopes or the tundra, few hunters spend more than a few days a year in upland game shooting. This is not the pattern, however, in waterfowl hunting. Rivers, sloughs, tidal areas, and marshes near Anchorage provide an abundance of birds. The better waterfowl shooting areas, which are dependably productive early in migration season, are those along the shores of the Bering Sea. Certain points, including the estuaries of rivers at such places as Dillingham, Port Heiden, and Izembek Bay, are well known for their production. These last three places are at a considerable distance from Anchorage, and although special cut-rate airplane flights are arranged to encourage the avid duck and goose hunter to consider at least a trip or two during the year to these remote points, it is not sufficient to bring many gunners together in those areas.

The black brant is considered at best only incidental to a day's shoot, according to a canvass of some 25 hunters in Anchorage. There was no evidence that they were even familiar with the best spots, had made any attempts at learning to call the birds, or were equipped with decoys.

It must be remembered that although these are the conditions now, with statehood every avenue of commercial profit is being developed. Therefore, thinking must not be along the complacent lines of letting well enough alone, especially where wildlife resources are concerned, even though game is not yet in immediate danger. In every instance where full understanding, good management, and practical restraint are lacking, these fine resources have dwindled, and in many places have disappeared. Game scarcity is already notable in some of the areas. In nearly every Alaskan center of mushroom growth, the result of the defense program or other stimulants, one must go far afield today to hunt game. Alaska can easily become a "have-not" state.

Alaska has already adopted a policy of tourist attraction, and tourism has shown particular momentum among hunters and fishermen. With the cessation of passenger boats a few years ago, the "look-see" tourist passing through the country merely to view its scenery and then travel on is now becoming a smaller portion of the trade. A substantial number of visitors now are those who want to enjoy the wildlife in an area where hunting and fishing are still highly productive. Game hunters in particular have quickly adopted the advantages of Alaska's rapid airline transportation. Facilities for air travel in Alaska have increased notably in the past ten years. A surprising number of persons are employed in air service in Alaska, as one notes coming into any small community with a landing strip, radio, or weather station. The air traffic is great enough at times to tax the number of people servicing the flights, which indicates that it is likely to increase in the future.

From the Cold Bay airfield, the aggressive hunter can fly in for local hunting. It is but a few miles from Izembek Bay, where vast feeding areas for waterfowl can be reached. (See Fig. 10.) Fall concentrations of brant are common. This airfield is now in the process of being greatly improved. Present plans indicate that the resident population will increase, and in an area where self-sufficiency will be sorely taxed. Since recreation is limited to what the area affords, hunting the brown bear and waterfowl and fishing will be a natural outlet.

The prospect of a gradually increasing change in many of the isolated brant areas like Izembek does not offer insurmountable obstacles to adequate protection. It is better to take thrifty steps now, before barriers of wasteful practices, prejudices, or habit prohibit sound and effective regulation. The atmosphere for attaining the best management plan is good.

Baja California

At the southern limits of the brant's migration one finds, in addition to the native Mexican hunter, the American who has become an enthusiast. At considerable cost and inconvenience, he will make an occasional trip to their wintering grounds to have a few days' sport.

Brant hunting is not a common recreation of the Mexican people. Only an occasional Mexican is a true hunter, and the small number of Mexicans who make a career of using, selling, or bartering the brant they kill do so under several limitations: lack of funds to buy an automatic or pump gun and ammunition, and little market or barter value. Consequently, their weight has little influence in the total harvest.

Under the natural restraints placed on the taking of brant in Mexico, there would perhaps be a greater drain on the total numbers if a larger market existed. A successful hunt resulting in a sizable bag can only add to the problem of the native because so few people can buy his kill. As for the occasional out-of-country traveler or tourist as a market, unless the bird is dressed, few visitors are prepared to cope with plucking, dressing, and cooking any waterfowl.

Only an economic upturn in living conditions in Baja California will change the situation to any appreciable degree. The black brant might be used as food by local people were ammunition and transportation readily available, but although living conditions have improved in recent years, they will not affect the general population for some time. The most aggressive hunting continues to be that of the occasional transient who comes for the sport.

There is evidence of this at San Quentin, the northernmost haven of the brant in Baja California. In the past decade, a few enlightened brant hunters from nearby United States cities have enjoyed these birds yearly on a thrifty and prudent basis. The hunting seasons in the winters of 1958 and 1959 were extremely disheartening to them, because other countrymen have entered these waters and, with poor ethics and high-speed boats, are now selfishly exploiting the brant of this area. There are local irritations raised by unsportsmanlike disregard for reasonable bags. A recent hunter admitted that he and one companion took 134 in a day's shoot. If this sort of aggressiveness is continued, the result can only be the disappearance of brant from that area.

Under current conditions, the Mexican sportsman and the native resident on the bays and lagoons will have little influence upon the total populations but tourism may be a serious influence.

The California Harvest

Among the hunters in California one finds the purist, who enjoys brant hunting as he does no other sport. The lagoons and bays are few but offer many enjoyable days to the dedicated brant enthusiast. Morro and Humboldt bays are favored areas. Since Humboldt Bay is of considerable size, it offers the best sport for the species in California. On the ocean side of the bay, a long barrier beach of sand barely above sea level is the crossing point of the brant from the open ocean to the inland waters. It is a common rendezvous for gunners throughout the open season. It is a place where the hunter, the naturalist, and the person of esthetic bent can return again and again to see the numerous flocks enter and leave the bay. Hunter activity here is reflected in the harvest records of California. It usually provides the greatest amount of sport to the brant hunter. It is the last area of rendezvous of the northward migrating brant concentrations in California and is often productive as the open season ends.

Oregon

Reference to Chart 3 will show the few areas they frequent in Oregon. Of the five available bays, only the two northernmost, Netarts and Tillamook, hold small segments of the migration each year, and in recent years the number has been dwindling. The presence of brant in the other three areas varies from year to year. Shooting has therefore been of little interest to the aggressive hunters, and only a few dedicated brant enthusiasts have launched their spreads of decoys behind the dunes. The largest concentrations are made up of the northbound migrants returning from Mexico and California. These usually occur after the hunting season has closed. Currently, national publicity has brought added pressures to an area not adapted to exploitation.

Washington

Washington waters usually favored by brant include several areas. Only Willapa Harbor attracts brant to the ocean coast. Grays Harbor, though similar in conformation, has lost its earlier attraction. The open waters of Dungeness Bay and harbor and the Strait of Juan de Fuca, particularly near Smith and Minor islands, are the haven for a considerable number of brant. The inland waters of Puget Sound and adjacent areas, Padilla and Samish bays, are generally visited by sizable flocks. But in the winters of 1958 and 1959 the birds were almost absent. On these bays a few hunters on privately owned points or sandspits account for a large part of the kill. One small state public shooting area on March's Point near Anacortes provides some sport for the public. The open-sea shooters, using an anchored boat and a large fleet of blocks, have occasional good days. The annual take is accounted for by a small group of perennial brant hunters. Many of the addicts are shoreside dwellers in this area, and they eagerly await the annual visitations of this sea goose.

The big cities, too, provide a few enthusiasts who look forward to the late winter season, their last chance to shoot waterfowl until the following October. An example of the persistence of the brant hunting enthusiasm came to my attention recently. Joshua Green, a pioneer of Seattle in his ninety-fifth year, made a perfect kill. His chauffeur, making a retrieve in a small boat, fought wind and sea for half an hour. This seemed a long time to Mr. Green and when he again downed a brant he elected to row out and retrieve his own bird. This took half an hour too. On returning home, he asked his nephew: "Was this a wise thing for me to do?" He is again awaiting the opening of the brant season.

Vancouver Island

The eastern coast of Vancouver Island, stretching from Nanaimo to Campbell River, has been noted as a late spring feeding ground of the black brant. In making contacts along this coast, I was surprised to

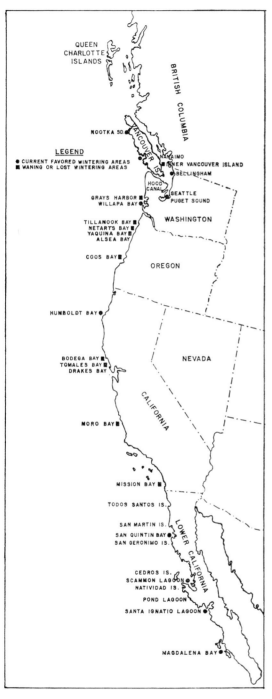

Chart 3. Pacific Coast wintering areas, showing increasing disuse of areas formerly favored by black brant.

learn how many people were deeply interested in black brant, far out of proportion to the numbers found elsewhere along their flyways.

This interest seems to stem from the fact that waterfowl hunting is quite limited because of the absence of puddle ducks. Despite a coastal shelf along much of this reach suitable for brant, there are very few shallow bays, marshes, and river estuaries that would harbor the puddle ducks in abundance. Most of the sea ducks seen are unappealing—the scoters, scaup, or golden-eye. The arrival of the black brant is eagerly awaited and a large number of men and boys respond to the opportunity to bag a goose.

A broad cross-section of people of various trades, skills, crafts, and professions participate in the sport, including loggers, farmers, teachers, and doctors. Most of the inhabitants live near the beach line. The populated flatlands at the base of the nearby hills are narrow enough so that everyone is familiar with the sea and uses it. It is the place where they picnic, camp, hike, and swim. It is also where they fish for trout and salmon. When the black brant swing into this portion of their yearly orbit usually in late December or early January, they are welcomed with enthusiasm. Hunters set up their spreads of decoys as long as regulations permit. The promontories, islands, and sandspits favored by brant are well occupied.

Brant also visit the western shores of Vancouver Island at many of the bays and lagoons such as Nitinat and Nootka Sound, but gunning pressure is limited as there is a sparse human population and access to the area is difficult.

The International Waterfowl Treaty regulations based on the migratory habits of the brant usually grant to British Columbia a later hunting season than in other Pacific coastal areas. In past years, the open seasons have been extended into late February. After the hunting season ends here, concentrations of the birds hit a peak. Soon there is evidence that the final flights in the northward migration are under way.

Even in mid-April, when the weather can be miserably raw, northward-straggling groups of black brant—harbingers of the nesting season will already have returned to Bristol Bay. In some years, drift ice may be pressing southward from the Bering Sea until ships passing through Unimak Pass are menaced, but forerunners of the black brant flight may already have put in their appearance on the tundra.

HUNTING THE BRANT

After the early harvest in Alaska, brant hunters are active in mid-winter from the west coast of Vancouver Island to the lagoons of Baja California. Their greater success comes first on the southern end of the orbit and later as the migrating birds return to California, Oregon, Washington, and British Columbia.

To hunt them successfully, the hunter must have good equipment, a boat that will withstand considerable seas, a good set of decoys, good heavy weather gear, and a gun of good carrying power. Here the concentrations do not compare with Alaskan habitats. Such hunters understand the sea, do not carp at weather, and have persistence and skill, of which "calling" is of importance. One of this group would need little encouragement to hunt, other than the presence of black brant passing some headland or using some back bay or lagoon. He knows that when brant arrive, the weather will be changeable during the hunting season, and that he must be punctual, because the stage of tide in most waters will have much to do with his success.

The usual place of hunting is a promontory, narrows, or offshore island or sandspit. Some of the best areas are productive of sport for only short periods each day, as the tides are at a level that prompt the brant to fly. A few sandbars or sand islands may contain only an acre or two of area, yet are the favored destination of brant from miles away. It is such meeting places that the stateside hunter seeks. Unfortunately, they are few and the birds instinctively drawn to them are often met by heavy gunfire. Such places, if not too isolated and difficult to reach, are persistently hunted, and the birds' eventual wariness is the only reason that heavier tolls are not taken.

Most brant hunters are interested both in these special birds and in their own skill. This includes the best knowledge of the tides and the brant's habits, the placing of the decoys, the concealment and camouflaging of the blind, and calling. They likewise have a devoted interest in seeing that brant return again and again to their havens.

The "shooter" has little of this in his make-up. It is a common pattern to see a blind, especially when the site is privately controlled, occupied steadily when brant are flying by replacement of some of the gunners. In this way, certain promontories have produced fifteen to

twenty limits in a day's shoot. The year's take in some instances runs
to several hundred from a single blind.

Hunting pressure on brant in the Pacific coastal states is unpredict-
able, but potentially it is surely destined to increase. Gun-minded people will be inclined to shoot wherever the chance is offered. Unreason-
able pressure on a species can build to explosion point from promotion
and exploitation. Commercialism, contests, publicity, and where-to-go
instructions released by business houses or community programs are a
modern and unwelcome trend. In many instances, species frequenting
local areas have been wiped out by these unrestrained publicity tactics. I know of localities, for example, where sage grouse, band-tailed
pigeons, and geese have been extirpated. Promotional publicity is a
good tool of management only when overabundance and its related
difficulties require a reduction of numbers.

Use of Decoys

The most effective hunters have long recognized the advantage of
decoys. Because brant are best attracted by a large fleet of blocks, the
hunter has the tedious task of carving the decoys from western red
cedar, a wood that is buoyant and easy to work. Because of the limited
market for brant decoys, few suppliers are found. Most of the blocks
are oversized with exaggerated necks, an astute imitation of brant as-
symetry in the water. The extra size of the decoys might make them
more visible to passing brant, a trick discovered early in brant shooting in the Puget Sound area, which might have been copied from the
Indians' shooting techniques. They, too, used the sandspits, bars, and
sandy shoals for decoys when the white man's guns became available.
The white man learned that he did not have to refine the brant decoys
at all. Like the Indian, he has used a fleet of crude blocks which, when
used by a practiced caller, often resulted in the decoyed birds' passing
over the stool several times and ignoring the gunfire.

In the Pacific coastal states and British Columbia areas, decoys of
both Indian and other craftsmen's designs are available; the former are
often found in antique shops and sell at collectors' prices.

Setting up a stool of decoys requires knowledge of brant's habits,
tidal ranges, and time of the desired level. In many localities, the
shooting opportunities are often best at high tide but in other areas
ebbing tides are more favorable. The areas to which the brant may be

expected to fly cannot be predicted. Local observations are generally the basis for hunter success. (See Fig. 11.)

As I have mentioned before, the black brant have a peculiar call. In decoying these birds, hunters make many attempts to imitate them. It appears that the pitch of the call is probably very important, and each person who attempts calling has a different approach. When the birds are within hearing distance, I have had considerable success in decoying them by giving a quiet call that sounds something like this: *quertúk quertúk quertúk,* repeated rapidly and pitched higher than my normal conversational voice. It seems to be a call of assurance. It is very effective over decoys; it comes very close to the rolling call of the black brant as they fly in over the bay, particularly when they are greeting their fellows before settling down on the water.

Batterson, who is especially adept at calling most wildlife, uses the following call vocabulary which can best be described as follows: *kr-r-r-ruck, kr-r-r-ruck, kr-r-r-ruck.* It is done with a trilling of the tongue and perhaps the intonation, inflection, and pitch are more important than the exact reproduction of what the brant is apparently saying to its fellows. A miscue in the choice of brant words may be interpreted by them as impaired speech.

Wesley Batterson has had broad experience in handling them as captive geese and in hunting the birds, using a trilling call. It is produced by placing the tongue against the back of the upper teeth. The pitch should be high, but no higher than can be voiced with ease. The symbol to use in imitating the brant's call can best be spelled as a trilling *tirrr, tirrr,* repeated twice—the higher-pitched syllable first and long, the second made at a lower pitch, but shorter. The tongue should vibrate or trill for a full second's duration, then an instant's pause should be followed by the lower trill. This should be repeated clearly when small flocks or stragglers seem to be interested in decoys. There is no substitute for being in brant territory to practice in the imitation of their calls, but improvement can come from hearing an expert call. It is an aid in hunting and when mastered it is a thrill to have good reponses.

Scull- or Sneak-boats

The use of specialized boats to take waterfowl, a practice that permits the gunner to use his weapon more effectively, can be traced back to the beginning of recorded gunning. In Europe, particularly England, the punt gun of large bore has always been one of the accepted tools of hunting. It is usually mounted on a boat that is propelled by an oar extending through the transom at the stern of the boat; the oar, manipulated like a propeller, moves the boat forward. Unlike sculling with two oars, this method permits complete concealment of the operator. This type of boat was quite common at the beginning of the century in various parts of the United States, particularly on the coastal waters and in some of the marsh and lake areas. Here it was known as a sneak-boat or scull-boat (see Fig. 12).

These boats were of two kinds: the single person scull-boat for the lone hunter, and the larger scull-boats, which provided room for two or three shooters in addition to the operator. These were generally used for hire. Some of the boats used in the Northwest in the early 1900's and until they were outlawed in 1913 were as much as eighteen feet in length and with a breadth of sixty inches. All scull-boats were designed to present a most deceptive appearance when approaching a flock head-on, the usual strategy in working up to a raft of resting puddle ducks. This was accomplished by having a very low stem piece barely extending above the water; the foredeck sloped upward to a shield or screen that was provided with small apertures through which an observer could look undetected.

In California they have continued to be a most efficient aid in taking waterfowl, particularly black brant. Article 2, Section 3681 of the California Game Code limits the use of scull-boats to Saturdays, Sundays, Wednesdays, and the opening and closing days of the season, in Fish and Game districts 8 and 9; but they seem to be unrestricted elsewhere in the state. Morro Bay currently harbors numerous scull-boats, several of which have recently been built. This indicates that they are an accepted aid and not restricted in use.

Offshore Floating and Fixed Blinds

Another practice that is gaining momentum is the utilization of offshore blinds, some of which are fixed structures made of piling and timbers with adequate platforms above high tide, offering shelter and concealment for the hunters. Many of these are far from the shores. The usual practice is to place decoys in the water close to the structures and in this way increase hunting efficiency, particularly for black brant.

Floating structures camouflaged by the use of burlap or reeds and cattails permit the entry of a boat in full concealment. Placed offshore, these aid the gunner materially (see Fig. 13). Many fixed blinds are located on favored spits or headlands where brant are known to pass close by (Fig. 14). In some places, these may be occupied almost continuously during the legal hunting season. In most situations, both the use of decoys and attempts at calling add to the advantage of these prime locations.

EFFECT OF GUN PRESSURE

I have observed that the black brant on wintering waters will drift into a favorite situation in some bay or backwater, appearing to establish themselves there for a considerable period of time. Based upon the full year's activity, however, the time is relatively short. Batterson, who has lived on the Oregon coast throughout his life, intimates that the black brant occupying a definite bay or inlet might be called a "communal" flock, which persist in that area, learn the routines that satisfy their physical needs and then follow this pattern. He mentions that they will remain until molestation forces them to leave the area entirely. Heavy hunting pressure often causes such a shift.

For example, persons setting up a stool of decoys on a favorite spit or sandbar, and shooting there persistently, will soon find that the black brant have occupied another part of the bay, avoiding the hazardous area or leaving in a search for other sanctuary. When this occurs, the only shooting that can be expected is provided by the arrival of brant unfamiliar with the local hazards. The shooting becomes spasmodic and unproductive as they, too, learn of the menace. Bars heavily shot early in the year may be barren for the remainder of the season. There are a few exceptions, where areas have an unusual appeal or promontories or barrier spits force brant to pass nearby and afford good gunning because these natural passageways offer entrance to favored or productive feeding waters.

Excessive gun pressure in such special areas is a serious threat to the welfare of black brant. The areas they prefer, such as sandspits, sandbars, or loafing shoals exposed at extreme low tide, are not numerous. Their exclusive use of a few key areas is essential in perpetuating the annual visitations of brant along our coasts. In Europe, gun pressure is reported as a critical situation and simple yet practical adjustments in brant hunting regulations may prevent similar menaces here.

PROBLEMS IN WATERFOWL MANAGEMENT

Thrifty custodianship of all our natural resources is a public duty. It is difficult to put forth such detailed guidelines that all phases of management are completely clarified. There are some principles of basic advice, however, which, if followed, will help prevent America from becoming a have-not nation.

Errors in Identification of Brant

The confusion in identifying black brant is general among the hunting fraternity, even in areas close to the birds' coastal habitat. In the Willamette Valley in Oregon, some hunters mention brant shooting when they are really referring to the smaller Canada (*Branta canadensis leucopareia*). Perhaps some of this confusion comes from the fact that the dark geese are scientifically classified as *Branta* and readers of waterfowl publications confuse the species. Even in habitats unsuited to the marine goose, where perhaps not even a single record of a sea brant can be found, hunters will vehemently insist that they shoot brant.

The confusion over waterfowl identification is a real management problem. In this day, since so few people are familiar with the size, silhouette, special habitats, or habits of species, waterfowl cannot be regulated by the management refinements that are needed. There is a concern now over the status of the redhead and the canvasback. It appears that the female redhead is less abundant than the male, so an annual yield cannot be forecast by dividing the total population equally into paired groups and thus arrive at a probable yield. A balance might be attained in time if the hunters were selective, taking approximately twice as many males as they do females.

But such a balance is impractical even to suggest. When waterfowl approach their blind, many hunters do not know whether they are shooting redheads or other species; to them, a duck is a duck. Even the size of the bird has little to do with the gross errors that are apparent in identification. Recently a gunner brought a whistling swan to a home economics kitchen in Portland, and his wife sought a recipe for preparing a goose. An alert gunner, sitting in a blind with the governor of a western state a few years ago, used strong action in pulling the latter's gun down as he took aim at a whistling swan. The governor's subsequent public statement was, "A man ought to be permitted a few honest mistakes." There is little similarity between a goose and a whistling swan. Such absurd errors indicate that a broader educational program is needed, with perhaps an identification test as a requirement to procure a license. This step must be taken eventually to safeguard waning species.

Importance of Age-Class Survival Differential

Because of the low reproductive yield of these birds, common sense dictates that the management of the species must be on a refined basis, and that inventories dealing with total numbers are perhaps not as significant as an inventory of reproduction for each year. Hansen and Nelson (1957) indicate that mortality rate for adult birds based on direct recoveries under a banding study is 21.8 per cent, compared to a rate of 45.4 per cent for young birds. If the annual yield of young is small, such a mortality would surely affect total numbers in a few years.

Whether this pattern is consistent year after year would be important in formulating management plans. If these rates of mortality are quite stable, adjustments in management might allow more of the small annual crop of young birds to reach the mating and breeding stage and thus bolster the productive segment of the species. For example, if the mortality rate for immature birds based on direct banded recoveries is approximately 45 per cent, and if the shooting season is continued into the period in which the adult mated birds are still harvested on the northern end of their orbit in such places as Humboldt Bay, California, and in Oregon, Washington, and British Columbia, then the attrition of the flocks must be twofold. If continued indefinitely, the mortality rate can cause a very rapid downward trend in population.

There is evidence that the immature birds of the year, probably because they are not wary and respond particularly to decoys and the skilled caller, come more readily within the range of the gunner than the adults. In years of good reproduction, their numbers are obviously reduced out of proportion to the total number of brant in an area. When few immature brant enter the harvest, it may well mean a poor reproductive season.

The second weak link in this chain of events is the continuation of the harvest at a time when the paired birds are likely to be the majority at the northern end of their winter's orbit before flying across the north Pacific to their nesting grounds. Removing one of a pair means that a second mate must be sought; and this will delay the hatching of a brood for another year. If both birds of a pair are removed, another segment of the total population has been wiped out forever, and it can be replaced only when the surviving immature birds reach maturity, mate, and complete their orbit to the nesting grounds.

Improved management of brant does not mean that stricter hunting control is the simple solution. Habitat preservation and a better knowledge of the brant's life story are even more vital.

9

Current Management

One of the most useful steps taken by the cooperators in the study of the black brant, particularly by the U.S. Fish and Wildlife Service personnel in Alaska and the staff of the California Game Department in past years, has resulted from the banding of more than 10,000 black brant.

Harvest Data

The more active period when this work was carried out was between 1949 and 1953, with a lessened area-wide tempo of recent date. Approximately 900 bands have been recovered from this series of banding studies (Table 5). Roughly 10 per cent of those affixed have been recovered from the young birds banded on the nesting areas and from the few adults banded on the wintering areas of California. (See Figs. 15, 16, 17.)

It is impossible from the Hunter Kill Mail Surveys conducted to trace the history of each band affixed. In fact, many more bands are found than reach the recording office. These may be kept as mementos of a hunting trip, and there are records of both bird bands and fish tags having been fashioned into ornamental jewelry, such as watch chains, watch charms, pocket pieces, and so on. There is also evidence that hunters may purposely retain bands, particularly if they do not want to show higher game kills than other members of the hunting fraternity. It is more than a reasonable assumption that from some productive areas few or no bands are recovered for scientific evaluation.

Direct response from active biological workers, however, is very effective. An example is found in the recent return of fourteen bands from brant recovered in the U.S.S.R., particularly from the northern Siberian coast. Chart 4 shows the widely separated recoveries on the vast East Siberian sea coast and islands, evincing the thoroughness of those workers.

TABLE 5

RECORDS OF BANDED BRANT
California, 1949–54

Area	A ♂	A ♀	I ♂	I ♀	AU	IU
Take in Humboldt Bay						
1949	0	0	1	0	0	3
1950	8	5	5	16	15	21
1951	3	4	8	5	16	17
1952	1	4	3	7	9	7
1953	3	1	0	0	0	0
1954	3	5	0	0	0	0
Totals	18	19	17	28	40	48
Take in Other California Areas						
1949	0	0	3	2	0	4
1950	15	9	25	34	31	47
1951	6	9	19	14	33	50
1952	4	5	18	15	34	29
1953	4	3	0	0	0	0
1954	9	19	0	1	0	0
Totals	38	45	65	66	98	130
Grand Total	56	64	82	94	138	178

A. L. Nelson, with his staff at the Patuxent Wildlife Research Center of the United States Department of the Interior, has provided the material that permits a detailed breakdown of the recovery records of 345 black brant taken on the Pacific Coast. These are recoveries processed since January 1, 1955. Table 6 carries highlights of the banding recoveries, but interpretation of the data must take into account date of the recoveries. For example, the return of bands from the small number of birds banded in 1959 was recorded only twice for a total of 0.6 per cent. The recovery in subsequent years may add to this list in proportion to the number affixed. It is helpful to know that birds may retain bands for six years or more. The banding returns indicate that the life span of the black brant is probably quite long. This is often true with birds that produce small broods. Band-tailed pigeons, which produce only one young per year, have long life spans.

These records show a predominance of adult birds in the kill, further supporting the suggestion that life spans are relatively long, although the hunting season may be timed to affect mated brant predominantly. Immature birds are nearly absent in the hunter's bag in some years. Close scrutiny of the table shows no wide contrast of har-

vest involving sexes. The sex records of the adult birds indicate that both male and female are taken in approximately the same proportion, and this condition also holds among the immatures. Hence disproportion in sex as a factor in reproduction is probably not a threat to survival, if these figures are a true cross section of conditions. Annual reproduction has its foundation in the number of mated pairs that reach the tundra nesting areas. It is doubtful if mated pairs make up 50 to 60 per cent of the total brant numbers. A large proportion of the brant dally too long in the areas of winter concentration to take an active part in the reproductive season. When one visits the nesting ground, one is struck by this realization, because there the number of mated pairs with goslings falls far short of what is considered to be the productive flock. When anticipating yield, we have generally referred to the total brant numbers. There is an inclination also to expect optimum

TABLE 6

RECOVERIES OF BLACK BRANT
Frequency and Per Cent*

AGE AT BANDING			YEAR OF BANDING			SITE OF RECOVERY		
Classifi-cation	No.	Per Cent	Year	No.	Per Cent	Location	No.	Per Cent
Locals	46	13.3	1949	2	.6	Alaska	53	15.4
Adult	184	53.3	1950	56	16.2	British		
Immature	110	31.9	1951	78	22.6	Columbia	53	15.4
Unclassified	1	.3	1952	93	27.0	California	152	44.0
Local and			1953	48	13.9	Colorado	1	.3
nestling	4	1.2	1954	68	19.7	Mexico	36	10.4
						Oregon	4	1.2
						South Dakota	1	.3
						Washington	38	11.0
						Russia	7	2.0
Total	345	100.0		345	100.0		345	100.0

MONTH OF RECOVERY			YEAR OF RECOVERY		
Month	No.	Per Cent	Year	No.	Per Cent
00	3	.9	1953	2	.6
01	119	34.5	1954	30	8.7
02	94	27.2	1955	88	25.5
03	18	5.2	1956	118	34.2
04	1	.3	1957	76	22.0
05	4	1.2	1958	30	8.7
06	5	1.4	1959	1	.3
07	20	5.8			
08	2	.6			
09	6	1.7			
10	19	5.5			
11	9	2.6			
12	41	11.9			
94†	4	1.2			
Totals	345	100.0		345	100.0

* Processed from band recoveries from 1955–59.
† Unclassified.

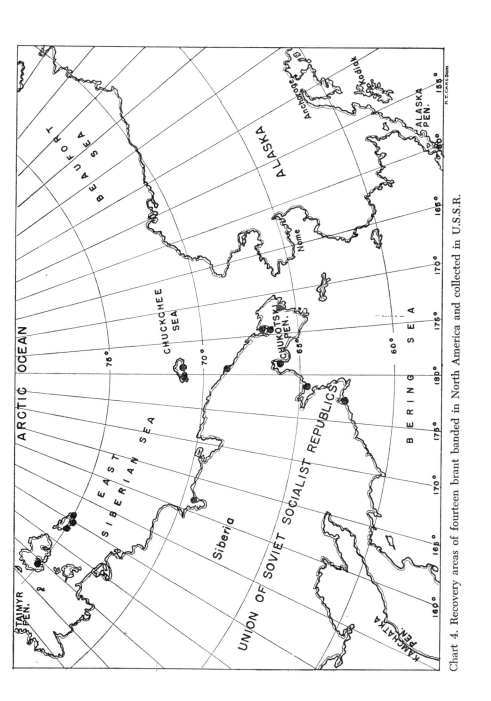

Chart 4. Recovery areas of fourteen brant banded in North America and collected in U.S.S.R.

brood survival, which does not appear to be consistent with the facts. Optimism about the size and stability of annual yields therefore seems inappropriate.

The records of band recoveries and harvest data show clearly that Humboldt Bay, California, is a center of concentration. As the birds migrate southward, some linger here for awhile. Many concentrate in the area in mid-winter, and finally, as the northward migrating brant approach on their drift toward their nesting grounds, a third period of occupancy develops. As a result, the hunters of California have been particularly successful in the Humboldt Bay area. The data on harvests, including the combined total harvests of Humboldt, Tomales, Bolinas, Drakes, Morro, and Mission bays, indicate that approximately 50 per cent of the total kill of black brant is made in California. Of all the favored habitats, however, Humboldt Bay is by far the most acceptable.

This area, consequently, is a key situation in management. Even if harvesting regulations everywhere else are well balanced, inadequate management regulations at Humboldt Bay can be a serious menace to black brant if suitable refuge area is not provided. For the harvest here may influence the southward migrating birds, the winter residents, and the northward migrating breeding stock.

Since the Hunter Kill Mail Survey was not designed to pinpoint areas of actual recovery, a person who is interested in these data should not become confused by returns from some of the counties. For example, San Diego County, California, shows a return of 193 brant, yet this is not one of the areas of heavy brant take. The hunters from this area are brant minded, and they range widely, hunting on the coastal areas of California. There are a considerable number of dedicated brant hunters who enter Mexico, hunting on San Quentin Bay, Scammons Lagoon, and other rendezvous; many of the San Diego returns, therefore, may be of this origin.

These references are made only to indicate avenues of approach to the problems of determining distribution, areas of brant kill, pressures on the species, influence of seasonal nature, and many other related facts, which would make our knowledge of brant habits far more acute. The black brant concentrate in just a few key areas and are now obviously in fluctuating supply. A sharply defined record program seems possible and timely and would simplify management while giving it a greater opportunity for success.

Evidence of the harvesting of mated birds in the northern part of the hunting range during the winter months is found in the work of Hansen and Nelson (1957). They report that R. H. MacKay, checking 383 brant in hunter bags in 1956 in British Columbia, found only thirteen juveniles. This could mean that reproduction was at a a low ebb, which seems to be reflected in the recently low levels of brant throughout its Pacific coastal range. This, coupled with other information, may spell out at least a partial reason for the fluctuating trends.

TABLE 7

BLACK BRANT—HUNTER KILL MAIL SURVEY DATA
1953, 1954, 1955, 1957

	COUNTY	TOTAL BRANT REPORTED
California	Del Norte	2
	Humboldt	226
	Mendocino	6
	Sonoma	10
	Marin	11
	Solano	42
	Alameda	5
	San Francisco	1
	Monterey	5
	San Luis Obispo	10
	San Diego	193
Oregon	Tillamook	80
	Lincoln	13
Washington	Whatcom	3
	Skagit	8
	Snohomish	14
	Clallam	42
	Jefferson	3
	Pacific	7
	Wahkiakum	4
	Cowlitz	7

Most of the hunters along the Pacific coast look back with satisfaction on the years 1952 and 1953, when the birds were most abundant and harvests were good. From their observations on local areas in recent years, practically all agree that the black brant are seriously fluctuating in abundance, that they were at their lowest level in 1959, and that there is need of a thorough study covering their entire range, with the objective of providing a better management plan to insure their perpetuation.

The British Columbia records seem to show that mated birds are more abundant in that locale as the annual hunting season ends. Birds born the previous year do not arrive until late in the winter and early spring, so the number killed represents a small proportion of their total numbers. Besides the obvious evidence that mated birds are consistently the first brant to reach the northern part of their winter range before taking off to the nesting grounds of the Alaskan coast, it seems logical to expect them to appear in the late hunting season everywhere when it continues into February. Brant of this age class are hurrying northward to be on time for nesting, whereas the nonbreeders may lag behind and course through the same orbit at a later date. On June 11, 1959, I observed two black brant of undeveloped plumage at Hudson Point in Port Townsend harbor in Washington. These birds had lingered long after several hundred brant had left the area in late April and early May. Birds of sexual immaturity feel no urgency in a time schedule. They have greater choice in their movements, which results in a leisurely migration. They may be found as far south as Morro Bay in late May, although many of them do not leave the Puget Sound–British Columbia areas until the early weeks of June.

These are all factors to be remembered in management. The situation can be determined by sampling for a few consecutive years. If the evidence offers conclusive proof that age class and mated birds determine migration schedules, then a further search of body quality, which showed these brant to be in good flesh, might suggest a test of several short, late, open seasons to harvest unmated or immature rather than paired breeding brant. This would insure a more equitable division of the harvest, and safeguard to a greater degree the mated birds, whose reproductive potential is the basis for yearly increases.

RELATIVE ABUNDANCE AND FLUCTUATION IN NUMBERS

Hunters familiar with black brant in the early days of Pacific coast settlement refute all reports of general abundance of the species. Optimum levels have probably been long past and never comparable to other geese in numbers. In most recent years until 1960 each census showed substantial declines (see Table 8).

The late S. F. Rathbun, hunter, collector, naturalist, and state director of game in Washington State in the late 1920's, discussed this subject with me many times. He had determined Pacific brant were in low numbers in comparison with other geese. Alfred Leque of Stanwood, a source of hunting lore till his passing, commented on their relative scarcity in the days when few people were present to hunt them.

In my own experience in their range in the Pacific coastal states, I have no evidence of the brant's great abundance. The late James Moffitt, who from boyhood concentrated on their study, reported in his many surveys that the species was not phenomenally abundant, since

TABLE 8

TOTAL POPULATION CENSUS RECORDS, BLACK BRANT—
ALL AREAS PACIFIC COAST
1950–1965*

Year	Number
1950	180,000
1951	168,300
1952	167,170
1953	154,605
1954	132,295
1955	135,110
1956	109,765
1957	131,526
1958	125,939
1959	68,484
1960	†104,954
	††136,983
1961	174,765
1962	225,352
1963	140,025
1964	185,281
1965	165,770

* Annual waterfowl census: Canada, U.S. Pacific Coastal States, and Mexico cooperating.
† First report.
†† Adjusted report.

the total number of brant in his annual inventories in California usually ranged between thirty and forty thousand. In his years of active work, California was a favored winter haven for brant and, with Baja California, held the major portion of the winter population.

The combined census records of the species for all areas of the Pacific coast reveal the trend to be downward from 1950 to 1959. The count fell from 180,000 in 1950 to about 68,000 in 1959. During this period, hunters felt that 1952 and 1953 were the most productive of harvest success, which the published reports seem to verify. However, during this period the total brant population never reached 200,000—a number that must be considered small when applied to a species vulnerable to habitat conditions on a coastline several thousand miles in length. Brant reported in each census year do not have the same reproductive potential as do a comparable number in a species like widgeons or pintail ducks. Yearlings of the latter species will reproduce their kind. Brant will not breed until they are in their third full year. Ducks may bring off a brood of from five to nine usually. Records on brant indicate that five is unusual and two seems to be an average return.

The records of rapid increases in 1960, 1961, and 1962 present several enigmas in statistical calculation or simple reasoning. The 1959 count was about 68,500. Based on observations on the nesting ground, there is evidence that probably no more than 60 per cent of the total population are breeding and nesting brant. Sixty per cent of the total stock would produce approximately 20,500 pair. Their theoretical production at a yield of two maturing young per pair would increase the total flock to about 89,000. If the yield were higher and three young brant survived to be counted, the theoretical yield added to the stock available would be about 109,000. If we choose a hypothetical 70 per cent as the breeding stock in 1959, the potential yield would total about 116,500, considerably short of the 136,900 reported for the year 1960. These census calculations suggest several causes for the wide changes. The reproductive rate could have been, as suggested, well above the norm for black brant; or the excessive drop from about 126,000 in 1958 to 68,500 in 1959 might mean that census coverage was not complete enough to locate considerable segments of the species that year. The 1960–61 relationships corroborate this suggestion. Here the increase from about 137,000 to approximately 175,000—an increase of 38,000—seems a more realistic upswing in the light of brant potentials, although it, too, seems a phenomenal increase. Should such upward trends prevail for a few years, brant stocks will exceed any abundance records of the past. This seems to have occurred.

Figures for 1962 of 225,000 brant, although indicative of a very limited yield from the mated parent stock available, are the highest ever recorded. The 1963 census records complicate analysis further by reporting a drastic decline of approximately 40 per cent, to about 140,000. This is followed by the census for 1964 which accounts for about 185,000 brant, indicating a small increase apparently far below the productive potential, but the 1963 report of flooded nesting grounds in the Yukon–Kuskokwim area is a logical conclusion.

Records in 1965 attest to a small decline from the inventory of preceding years. A similar fluctuation in trends is notable and natural over the past fifteen years, as shown in Table 8. In considering the recent survey, the most significant observation rests in the distribution of brant. Six-sevenths of the total Pacific flyway population was in Mexico during the 1965 census program; with about one-seventh in the coastal states of Washington, Oregon, and California.

California in the early days of census in the 1930's reported as many as 40,000 birds. In recent years, the California brant population at census time during the open hunting season has been dwindling, and in 1965 only 3,372 brant were recorded.

There are several possible conclusions in analyzing these figures. First, the early January census may be taken before a large segment of the brant have begun their return from the wintering grounds. Second, habitat conditions north of Mexico may carry handicaps influenced by human activity that force the birds to seek more favorable seclusion and freedom from molestation; and, finally, we have been familiar with brant habits only over a few decades and this erratic drift may be a normal tendency.

In working for their perpetuation, however, adequate sanctuary in California and Mexico now looms more important than ever.

It is difficult to interpret exactly what may be forecast as management directives from the available census data. There is one basic guideline that should impress both hunters and responsible management agencies: Pacific black brant are a minority species. To keep them within reasonable margins of survival safety, they cannot be used extravagantly or carelessly.

The available data together with field knowledge are impressive from a management standpoint. They compel attention. Here is a species with a wide migratory range. It seeks isolation. It is relatively low in numbers. Its habits require extended and difficult travel by the census takers. Because of brant concentrations on open water, the airplane is the best mode of travel to reach their rendezvous. Yet airplane census taking has its serious difficulties. Brant will often rise long before the plane is in the best position for blocking the flock into suitable divisions for inventory purposes; thus it is often simpler to estimate total numbers from a fixed position where detailed scanning can be accomplished. There are probably fewer qualified aerial census takers than those who work from the land.

Airplane census work entails long flights, yet because of the gregarious habits of the brant, as well as the restrictions on census flights, a large segment of the winter concentrations may be overlooked. Census may be further complicated by weather. Ideally, the flights should be carried out almost simultaneously throughout the brant's winter range; a few days' delay may mean a shift in the concentrations and a large segment of brant may be absent from the search area. Brant may either be left out of a census entirely, or be enumerated twice. Facilities for carrying out an airplane census of brant are improving, however. Coordinated use of better communications and agency airplanes will eventually permit a one-day survey of the entire wintering areas of the species and much of the chance for error will be reduced.

Hunting harvest is perhaps the most easily controlled factor in the life of the black brant. It can be accomplished by restrictions of timing, length of season, and bag limits. The natural limitations, however, work toward a restricted kill. Hunting in the so-called good years of the early 1950's may have been an influence on the trend of succeeding years. It is obvious that the harvest during the past ten years has had little to do with the fluctuations, simply because the take of black brant generally with very few exceptions, has been almost negligible.

California records in 1955 show an estimated harvest of approximately 20,800 brant. Hansen and Nelson (1957), in summarizing the knowledge of harvests, calculate that this figure probably accounted for a mortality of approximately 29,000 brant, which would include the crippled or unretrieved birds and reduction in mated pairs. From information at hand, it is obvious that the bulk of the kill was in California, particularly Humboldt Bay, with the lesser harvest at Bolinas, Tomales, and Morro bays, and the total annual California kill was probably more than half of the harvest throughout the brant's orbit in the years of greatest abundance.

The kill figure for Oregon and Washington is much smaller, although there are a few key points in each area where considerable harvest occurs. A few favored areas on such places as Willapa and Padilla bays in Washington have produced sizable harvests, and even in the relatively poor year of 1957–58 one club, which exists solely for the shooting of black brant, took over 900 birds. A public shooting ground, maintained by the state of Washington in the same general vicinity, harvested less than 300 birds.

Fig. 15. Migration studies are aided by banding brant. Here a cannon is set. (*Photo by Robert Twist, U.S. Fish and Wildlife Service*)

Fig. 16. The cannon has been fired, and the brant are trapped in the net. (*Photo by Robert Twist, U.S. Fish and Wildlife Service*)

Fig. 17. The brant are rapidly removed from the net and banded with identification rings on one leg. (*Photo by Robert Twist, U.S. Fish and Wildlife Service*)

The harvest of brant in the several states and provinces varies greatly in number. This must always be so because of habitat conditions and the natural tendencies of the species. The brant management program has certain limitations in common with all waterfowl management under the treaty stipulations agreed upon by Canada, Mexico, and the United States. Hence the basic regulations must conform to standard procedures that can be applied uniformly, with the species' needs the foremost consideration. But the brant have been of limited interest to the majority of hunters, thus the harvesting regulations differ regionally, are still immature and parochial. Simple adjustments in control of harvests would be a wise action, anticipating growing handicaps to this goose and assuring a future for it.

Lack of attention to habitat is the second major influence on the perpetuation of the species. There are valid reasons why little attention has been given to the habitat throughout the orbit of the black brant. The waterway frequented by the species is like a cobweb in the sky. It occupies but a narrow strip of space, and the presence of the birds in any area, except on their breeding and nesting grounds, has the ephemeral nature of a shooting star. Here and soon gone, they leave behind few traces; and they are obvious only in the few places where they congregate at the southern end of their wintering sojourn, Baja California, in the northwest states and in British Columbia. Then they are gone again, phantomlike, over a vast stretch of ocean, to become real as they reach a rendezvous, the narrow tundral strip along the Arctic shores.

Because the brant have figured so little in localized areas of management concern, it must be assumed that the style, techniques, and hunting practices have simply evolved in each community where the brant are accustomed to visit. Thus hunting practices vary greatly from one portion of their range to another. The basic regulations of season and bag limits set under treaty influence are the only guide lines of control. In recent years a dangerous kind of uniformity has been developing. Many hunters, and managers as well, seem to consider it a sacrilege to leave something unharvested when there is no crisis of overabundance. Abundance is not a quantity that can be easily measured—the accounting of wild things does not have the accuracy of striking a bank balance, and there are no instruments for determining the fine lines of safety—thus waste and aggressiveness persist. It is basic in management that we should err chiefly on the side of conservatism, except where it is obvious that we are nearing optimum levels. But this is not the trend today, and for that reason we may quickly get our harvest out of balance on the less abundant species. In the frightening example of the band-tailed pigeon, which each year produces only one young per mated pair, there is no easy means of recovery once the brood stock has begun to dwindle. With the ring-necked pheasant, however, low levels in abundance might be raised quite rapidly by an artificial program of harvest adjustment and restocking; then the coverts may again yield satisfactorily.

In the case of the black brant, the time is now at hand when a more realistic viewpoint should be considered. Everything that man can do—this should be one of the first tenets of management approach. In many ways these are simple contributions, and logical in their simplicity when the life story of the black brant is considered. To have many of the wild things that we cherish, we must concede at least their basic needs, and it is just good common sense to recognize that the brant's habitat must be provided. They are not birds of extravagant demands. They require only a few favored spots and certain key conditions. Isolation is paramount. Their use of each segment of their orbit is quite refined. The several facets of their life which are still only partially understood deserve the close attention of all who are interested in the species' survival.

Here are a few thoughts that continually recur in a naturalist's mind. Are the birds that are taken in the delayed hunting season on the northern end of their winter orbit invariably the paired and parent stock from which this year's crop will develop? What is the true percentage of nonbreeding birds on the nesting grounds? Have we been multiplying too rapidly and not subtracting? Is the reproductive trend probably half of what we have generally expected from this goose? Brant have never been abundant: does this mean that their special requirements confine them in number as well as geographical area?

We are at the doorway of approaching the problem of the black brant, from the standpoint not of a management program but of a research and fact-finding program. Should this bird disappear, it will be the result of what mankind does or does not do.

10

Suggested Changes for Brant Survival

PROTECTION AND REGULATION OF ESKIMO NEEDS

The privilege of out-of-season harvests by Eskimos cannot be tolerated in dense centers of mixed population, such as Nome or Point Barrow or elsewhere. Wherever the natives come into contact with people not of their race there is a false stimulation to harvest. In the settlements of mixed population, the Eskimo has already begun to accept the way of life of the white man and his own culture is being diluted. New opportunities probably stimulate him to capitalize on his privileges, and in this he continually stirs up envy or irritation. The Northwest Indian in a like manner is jeopardizing salmon runs by fishing for salmon commercially on their spawning beds. The only place where the practices of self-preservation under the old culture are important is in the isolated parts of the Alaskan coast and tundra areas.

Management, therefore, can be simply attained by two actions: first, by setting the open season on waterfowl *when the birds are there;* and second, by defining areas of closed-season protection from Eskimo hunting where conditions jeopardize waterfowl survival.

In support of the first step, zoning may be necessary, as the early departure of waterfowl in the past years has reduced the food supply of the natives. When the season opens on the northern arctic shores in September, only a remnant of the waterfowl may be available. Hence an open season may be meaningless. The season should come after all the birds are on the wing, but not so late that none can be taken.

A survey of critical areas needing special attention is possible. The second step could be initiated by restrictions on the well-known troublesome centers of out-of-season depredations. The desirable goal should be to perpetuate the Eskimo families who tend to cling to the sea edge and tundra in many strategic places.

Whatever changes are made, it would be well to see that these truly unusual people of the northland retain as much as possible of their primitive culture. For example, the loss of the hunting privilege by the male Eskimo would be a serious blow to his pride. It would remove the most cherished right in his way of life, a right that the Eskimo wife or daughter has by tradition never enjoyed. It would rob the Eskimo man or boy of his confidence and self-respect.

Karl Kenyon of the research division of the U.S. Fish and Wildlife Service tells of an incident that supports the foregoing contention. One night a polar bear entered an Eskimo camp and the dogs became frantic, heralding his presence. This stirred the lone family to action, but in his frowsy and befuddled excitement the man could not find his rifle, and the bear departed unharmed. In a fortnight the same thing happened again, but this time the rifle was located and the bear was dropped practically in the barabara doorway.

The episode might normally be considered a success story, but this was not so. The mother gloried in needling her husband about the kill: he was no hunter, she said; he was lazy and could shoot polar bears only when they came up and asked to be killed. He couldn't even find his gun. If *she* were permitted to hunt, she would have killed the bear on its first visit. And (she claimed) she would have been the first Eskimo lady in all the arctic to kill a polar bear.

To the Eskimo man the loss of the hunting right and custom would be a blow to his pride and community dignity of crushing effect.

If at some time it developed that one species of waterfowl was becoming severely pressed—and this could occur here only in unusual situations—then it would be desirable to place practical and effective restraints on hunting. The black brant might be such a species because of its limited habitat. Yet it may be that the survival levels of the black brant are influenced, either directly or indirectly, far more by the several million citizens of the West Coast than by the handful of Eskimos on the northern tundra.

In the larger centers of trade on the tundra coast, where waterborne freight can be delivered to the door from our Northwest markets, a cylinder of rolled oats selling currently in the stores of the West Coast at 35 to 40 cents ranges from $1.05 to $1.20.

Stores well equipped to refrigerate their foods were selling bacon at $1.75 a pound, and most articles of everyday need were being offered at what appeared to be 100 per cent profit based upon original and transportation costs. These observations were made in 1958. The spread may be even greater today. Eskimos find local harvests of wild life important in their welfare.

Modern ways have affected the Eskimo adversely even in his transportation. The day of the kayak and the oomiak is almost gone. A few are seen around the camps, but power skiffs are now being used almost universally in this region. The mode of power is the outboard motor. The horsepower of the units has crept up steadily until most Eskimos try to procure a motor of from 25 to 50 horsepower whose gasoline consumption is extravagant. All these motors are of the two-cycle type, consuming from two to six gallons per hour. Gasoline costs one dollar a gallon. An Eskimo who sells his labor, furs, or fishes has little margin for living costs after he has used this type of equipment in producing his trade goods or labor. In the northwestern states, gasoline costs are about one-fourth of the price to Eskimos. What they receive for their fish is less than half of the value per fish caught in Washington or Oregon.

In the trading posts, the stock of rifle shells far exceeded that of shotgun shells. The mammal upon which the Eskimo depends is the seal. The rifle ammunition is stocked primarily for seal hunting, although a few Eskimos are successful in bagging moose or caribou on the inland edges of the tundra. In conversation with the Eskimos we learned that they depend more on much rapid shooting than on skill. The younger Eskimos, too, lack a sense of thrift: in their attempt to collect seals or walrus they follow the wasteful tactics of barrage shooting.

There is at present a native National Guard guided by military personnel. It was apparent that few of the latter were familiar with the wildlife resources of the area, and they were responsible for military training without perhaps giving consideration to the other aspects of Eskimo life. Possibly as important as training in tactical maneuvers and military discipline—or even more important if the natives are to survive on the tundra—is an understanding of the Eskimos' needs. The rifles and ammunition made available through the National Guard have been reported as a detriment to Eskimo welfare since there are rumors and evidence of wanton waste of seal and walrus as an end product of ample ammunition. Fay (1960) writes: "Many hundreds of tons of walrus hides and flesh are wasted annually merely to satisfy the demand for a few pounds of ivory trinkets." For that reason it might be suggested that personnel chosen to work closely with the natives be well qualified in observing the trend of the wildlife resources, and in familiarizing the natives with weapons and gear that are more productive and less wasteful.

I think I should tell of an experience that shows how civilization is hitting the land of the Eskimo. I saw a modern barbecue kit or rotisserie in operation at an Eskimo's camp. It had originally been fitted for electricity, but in the absence of electric power he had ingeniously converted it to a hand-crank operation, and was barbecuing whitefish over the charcoal. Obviously it had been a mail-order purchase and was the delight of the community. It was probably one of the most practical extravagances. But instead of burning imported bagged charcoal at from two to three dollars per pound, he could have used the local wood of the area at no cost at all. This is only one example of what is meant by helpful extension work among the Eskimos.

To a large degree we are trying to teach the Eskimo to live as we do. But our attitude should be reversed: we should try to improve the lot of the Eskimo by helping him to adjust to his own environment, and leave him in a habitat where he is extremely happy, but where the hazards of life can be more successfully met. This is possible if those whom we send to the tundra, to maintain a military liaison with the nomads, are skillful, ingenious, devoted, and persistent people.

A chain reaction of improvements could begin with as simple a step as developing the natives' skill with rifles. This would make their harvest afield more consistent and less wasteful, and the Eskimos themselves would certainly become more valuable in the present training program. Those in the native national guard who show adeptness and leadership could be detailed back to the communities to improve the general skill and pride in the use of guns.

RESTRICTIONS RECOMMENDED ON HUNTING AIDS

The naturalist-hunter whose career has been dedicated to protect the "great society" of wildlife may not have the materialistic viewpoint of many hunters. Bag limits, to him, are not nearly as important as skeins of brant seasonally sliding across a sunset sky and their cheering call drifting in over the waters. Suggestions on harvest techniques, therefore, should be evaluated solely on their contributions to the perpetuation of the species.

Decoys

Some limitation in the use of decoys, which have long been proven to be irresistible to small flocks or straggling brant, would prevent the well-equipped and aggressive hunter from using them in excessive numbers. Carl Wiedemann demonstrated this in Samish Bay in Washington forty years ago. He was one of the first to whittle out a flock of over 150 brant, and whenever he anchored his fishing skiff in mid-bay the sharp eyes and gregarious tendencies of the birds flying by several miles from his flotilla usually brought them into gun range. Others now find this a productive method.

The goal of good management, however, is not to await the day when heroics must be attempted but rather to have an orderly and satisfactory yield and the assurance that this fine sport can last indefinitely. This can be partially attained by insisting on smaller stools of brant decoys: twenty-five is adequate for good hunting yet does not have the drawing power of the larger numbers. Decoy restriction should therefore be considered in management.

Scull- or Sneak-boats

In the interests of good management there appears to be no justifiable reason for considering the use of the scull-boat to be a desirable practice. It is one of the added tools that make an equitable sharing of the crop of waterfowl impossible. It is another practice like "baiting" which more often favors a skilled and aggressive minority while the majority, often with lesser means, conforms to more conservative practices to find their sacrifices useless in perpetuating the very species they protect. If all waterfowl hunters were permitted to use scull-boats, most habitat for waterfowl would be untenable, resulting in a rapid decline in numbers. It is natural for an individual to reveal his fondness for a particular method of harvest. Trout anglers continually argue over the merits of bait and fly fishing. The manager of wildlife usually recommends the type of harvest based on local conditions that is best designed to harvest a crop and no more. The areas where wildlife is sustained today have been supported by this type of safe-guard. Brant without a refuge or sanctuary cannot continually face molestation on their feeding ground, despite earnest arguments to the contrary. A recent article (1964) extolls scull-boat hunting on the grounds that it requires exacting skill and therefore will not become a popular sport. In this western range a decade past, skiing was the sport of few people; today millions have mastered the skill. The use of scull-boats should be banned.

Offshore Blinds

In most instances, the use of a blind is a desirable part of the hunt-ing technique, but like other practices this should be regulated so as not to be a complete handicap to other hunters or a serious menace to the game being sought. One practice affecting black brant is that of building blinds far offshore and in a scattered fashion on the eelgrass beds, where no refuge or sanctuary areas are reserved for the birds. This results in a real handicap to their normal feeding tendencies. For that reason the use of blinds should be carefully scrutinized in man-agement plans and an attempt made to have their erection conform at least to the existing laws, which are now apparently overlooked.

The agency responsible for issuing permits for any structure in navi-gable waters is the U.S. Corps of Engineers, who have offices in many districts in the United States. Existing laws provide that all persons desiring to perform any work or erect structures in navigable waters must obtain the prior approval of the Chief of Engineers. This approv-al is normally granted in the form of a "Department of the Army Per-mit," which is issued by the district engineer in charge of the area con-cerned. In cases of minor works sufficiently removed from navigation channels so that no possible interference with navigation may result, procedures exist whereby permission may be granted in the form of a "Letter of Permission." The use of blinds of this nature is very common in California waters, and having noted their effect on brant in south Humboldt Bay particularly, I solicited information about them from the district army engineers at San Francisco, California. Their reply (a letter of January 19, 1959) outlines conditions under which structures in navi-gable waters are permitted, and ends with the following statement: "This office has no record of any permission being granted for hunters' blinds, such as you describe, in the South Humboldt Bay area."

Puddle ducks and even the diving ducks may not be seriously handicapped by offshore blinds, for these birds can resort to a wide range of waters, both marine and inland. Intimidation and aggressive hunting on the tidal flats and shallows of the few bays and lagoons acceptable to the brant, however, are particularly disturbing. These birds have no substitute havens to which they can withdraw.

Sanctuary Provisions

The life of each species has a well-defined pattern. Action that we may consider as a mere chance or an odd phenomenon, because we do not understand its purpose, is perhaps vital to the species' survival.

The persistent attempt of brant to leave the sea for solid ground, for example, is not a passing fancy. Most geese would drown if they were not provided with a fatty uropygial gland in the tail area to provide water-proofing. Its use is a simple process. Birds like the brant come ashore if possible and spend a period rubbing the fatty substance from this gland through their feathers. This protects them from the surge of the sea and makes them impervious to water. Loafing places are therefore very important for brant survival. This act cannot be thoroughly accomplished at sea, for there the underbody could not be properly treated. Even domestic ducks and geese spend hours daily to achieve this protection. The desperate need for freedom and sanctuary for brant to accomplish this now makes the establishment of havens of protection a vital necessity.

Batterson reports that goslings raised by poultry foster mothers, such as Plymouth Rocks or other steady brood hens, never develop the same waterproofing techniques as other geese, and if forced to remain in either fresh or salt water they will become waterlogged and drown in a few hours. I have had the same experience with mallards. Ducklings and goslings at birth are not able to waterproof themselves. In the first weeks of their lives they acquire some protection nestling under the breast of their mother. Eventually they mature to the point where it becomes a habit to force their bill across the oil gland and then through their own feathers. That self-oiling is effective and important for survival cannot be questioned.

Because human activity is a constant menace to the black brant throughout their wintering range, a possible solution might be to set aside a number of beaches and adjacent water areas that provide sufficient eelgrass beds to sustain them. It is known that some concentrations of brant amount to twenty or thirty thousand, and a considerable amount of space is necessary to meet the needs of so large a group.

There are at present four basic areas where a comprehensive program of refuge establishment would be especially effective in harboring the larger segments of the brant population. These are the Yukon–Kuskokwim delta; Izembek Bay, Alaska; Humboldt Bay in California; and the Black Warrior and Scammons lagoons in Mexico, the latter two actually being joined together to make one unit. These four areas offer space for comparatively large sanctuaries. The establishment of adequate refuge in Alaska has already been accomplished, and is dealt with in later paragraphs.

Consideration of smaller units has merit, but has not been emphasized here because brant perpetuation actually rests on these four key areas. That smaller units of sanctuary offer considerable promise, however, is to be found in observations made in such places as Tillamook Bay on the Oregon coast, Padilla and Samish bays in Puget Sound, Washington, and in recent observation on Hood Canal.

It has been the practice for long years past to shoot brant wintering in the upper reaches of Hood Canal, where it ends in the vicinity of Belfair. Favored spits and shoals exposed at low tides and the eelgrass beds wherever they become available in this area have been occupied by the black brant. A few years ago a small state beachside park on an area formerly set aside as an oyster seed reserve was established about four miles west of Belfair on the northerly shore of this arm of Hood Canal. This area had been heavily hunted, because it offered the type of conditions that brought the brant in periodically. With the establishment of the state park where all firearms are prohibited, this small area has become the sanctuary of the black brant, and here they can now live unmolested as long as they remain within its boundaries. The park includes beach line approximately a half mile in length, as well as adjacent offshore waters. In actual measurement this is a very restricted area, yet it does harbor and offer protection to the brant wintering here. A few years ago heavy hunting on a few spits—and this meant heavy boating activity, too—often drove waterfowl from the area. Now it is not unusual to see several hundred brant occupying these park waters and adjacent beaches in complete contentment. Now, too, hunting takes the skill of the caller and his ability to attract birds by the proper placing of decoys. He is also assured of brant remaining in the vicinity. Other relatively small refuge areas may be helpful in sustaining the sport on a sportsmanlike level.

This park area, which was created solely for the satisfaction of people, has inadvertently offered sanctuary to black brant and other waterfowl. This chance development, in an area that probably would not have been considered potentially productive by people in waterfowl management, suggests a plan for brant survival. A comprehensive survey of strategic recreational areas might isolate potential habitats for the brant. It would not be difficult to realize these habitats, and thus augment the basic protection offered by sanctuaries in the four key areas named above. This supplementary action would contribute much to the protection and perpetuation of the brant and add to the pleasure of nature lovers and hunters as well. Unfortunately, it has already been suggested that hunting of game in state parks of Washington should be a winter privilege. Senate Bill 384, asking this concession, failed in the Washington State legislature at the 1963 session.

Four areas are vital to the survival and perpetuation of the black brant. They are: (1) the nesting grounds along the Bering Sea coast, stretching from Nunivak and Nelson islands into Kotzebue Sound and adjacent areas—and of this stretch the Yukon–Kuskokwim deltas are the most vital for nesting waterfowl; (2) Izembek Bay, at the southern end of Bristol Bay and on the Bering Sea side of the Alaskan Peninsula, a premigration concentration area; (3) Humboldt Bay, California, a wintering haven; and (4) Scammons Lagoon, Baja California, which holds the greatest wintering concentrations.

The first and second areas are the major nesting and nurturing grounds for the species, and they may hold some of the birds for as

long as eight months of the year. They are in a range of little human
influence and parts of them should be so held indefinitely. Efforts to set
these two areas aside as the homing range of waterfowl have been un-
derway for several decades. There have been fluctuating tempos of action by the U.S. Fish and Wildlife Service and by individual conservationists. The first steps of significance came in 1942, when official action to withdraw these areas from the public domain were initiated. A
series of national events, such as the influence of military action in
Alaska, statehood for Alaska, and related episodes created varying climates for accomplishment. On December 7, 1960, the press of the nation released the information that Fred A. Seaton, Secretary of the Interior, had established three Alaskan wildlife ranges. Of importance to
waterfowl and to geese especially was the creation of the 1,800,000-
acre Kuskokwim National Wildlife Range, encompassing vital areas of
the Kuskokwim and Yukon deltas, and the 415,000-acre Izembek National Wildlife Range, the traditional premigration concentrating area
of the black brant.

This policy of waterfowl perpetuation insurance will be respected
throughout the entire length of the Pacific coast flyway. It is an example of timely custodianship in natural resource management, and the
decision of Secretary Seaton will be regarded by a grateful people
with increasing understanding as the years pass by. It preserves the
nesting and nurturing areas of waterfowl and also sets a precedent in
emphasizing that other key areas, vital particularly to black brant,
must now receive detailed management attention. The creation of adequate protection on Humboldt Bay, California, and Scammons Lagoon, Mexico, will round out the most effective basic management
program for brant. Humboldt Bay is the largest area between Alaska
and Mexico perferred by brant, and it has the essentials for wintering
brant, with its broad tidal areas and eelgrass beds. Strategically located, it is of critical value because of the many brant that must utilize it,
either late-wintering or pausing there in southward or northward migration. Yet because of the limited territory for the number of birds making this annual journey—in actual acreage it probably equals less than
2 per cent of the area of Izembek Bay, Alaska—it is sometimes filled to
maximum capacity. Moreover, its usefulness is being weakened by
human molestation (speed boats, commercial and private, churn the
waters of the bay continually), by the activities of the oystermen, and
by the persistence of the hunters. Hunters are more aggressive here

than in most brant hunting areas, for they use offshore blinds, some of which intimidate feeding brant, and scull-boats as well. Unfavorable conditions within recent years have driven the birds in desperation into adjacent pasture lands—an irritant to the farmers at the bay's margin. Adequate refuge area in the southern portion of Humboldt Bay should correct this problem without affecting economic and recreational opportunities unduly, since eelgrass is well distributed on other bay areas.

An area of satisfactory size in Mexico lies in the combined Black Warrior and Scammons lagoons, two interlocking lagoons that hold the greatest winter concentrations of black brant. At times perhaps 50 per cent of the total population will converge on these waters. The isolated parts offer the brant real protection; but danger could develop from a commercial practice that brings in oil tankers and other carriers to pick up unprocessed salt for ballast or commerce from the vast surface deposits. If these ships ever came with sea water ballast from some area where the eelgrass was diseased, releases of such ballast in Scammons Lagoon might spell the eventual doom of the eelgrass there. It is a menace that can be simply controlled by chemical treatment of water ballast, but one careless discharge of eelgrass-destroying spores or reproductive cells could affect the productiveness of this fine wintering ground. The Scammons Lagoon eelgrass is more vulnerable perhaps than in any other range, because of the practices involved and because of the sea water temperature, which is much higher and a better medium for parasitic infestation than in the other coastal habitats in Oregon, Washington, British Columbia, and Alaska. A real hazard exists, and in a situation where few other substitute habitats can be found.

NEEDED RESEARCH

The first to give momentum to Pacific Coast interest in the black brant was James Moffitt, whose articles in the *California Game Bulletin* in the early 1930's reveal the enthusiasm, persistence, and dedication of an individual working toward a definite conservation goal. His interest resulted in the annual black brant inventory, which has determined numbers rather than the details of brant's life history, and thus engendered a better general recognition of the species. This has no doubt stimulated a broader interest, which can now lead to effective management procedures wherever brant range. The increasing general interest and helpful attitude of the several management bodies, as well as the enthusiasm of the hunters, resolve the present as an ideal time for constructive action as management procedures vary greatly and do not meet current conditions.

There has been no orbit-wide coordinated effort to understand the needs of black brant. The research work carried on by the Alaskan personnel of the U.S. Fish and Wildlife Service has been outstanding in that area; particularly valuable has been the work of those few enthusiasts assigned to the hinterlands, for this has yielded much information on the travels and traditions of the species. The early work of C. E. Gillham, carried out under terrific handicaps of travel and living, pointed to the key problem areas and to the need for research. Alaska and California have produced dedicated workers but everything accomplished so far has gained its momentum chiefly from individual enthusiasm.

The time has now arrived for a carefully outlined, coordinated program, motivated by the game management agencies throughout the brant's orbit. The research work necessary to complete the task will involve very few workers. A complete survey of the potentialities of refuge areas should be the first step. A comprehensive analysis which pieces together the procedures that are vital to maintain the black brant at optimum levels should follow in the light of research findings. The goal is not to exclude the black brant from an annual harvest, but to provide a satisfactory division of this resource and harvest it on an orderly basis. Desperation, bred by the thought that we are dealing with a remnant species on the brink of extinction and must therefore employ heroic measures, often results in unnecessary and usually ineffective moves. The Pacific black brant is not in this plight. Adjustments in orbit-wide methods of nurturing and harvesting black brant offer the best approach to stability in numbers and habitat.

The coastal areas exclusive of Alaska favored by brant are few and extremely small. It would not be a long or tedious task to determine which might be set aside as havens for brant. To simplify the task, brant do not readily change habitats once they have found what both suits them and remains unchanged; it is the change that harasses them. Pintails or white-fronted geese, on the other hand, may quickly shift from one locale to another, leaving unoccupied a recently popular haven. Mendall (1958) has shown us how the ring-necked duck has drifted away from a portion of its midwest habitat to become well established in the northeast lake areas, particularly in Maine. This would not happen with the black brant. If they can be offered a small margin of protection in their traditional habitat where eelgrass and sea lettuce flourish, they will come again and again to the same feeding and loafing grounds.

No true picture of the brant's utilization of their feeding areas can be acquired immediately after the birds arrive each fall, because gun pressure on waterfowl drives them into safer, more isolated areas. Only after hunting has ceased and several weeks of complete protection have passed can the use pattern be established. A survey then may reveal many small suitable areas for sanctuary that would contribute much to brant survival. But deference to human activity must be a part of such a program. Brant are not entirely timid of people, but they will not tolerate continual molestation. Their future rests first on adequate sanctuary in four key areas: the Yukon–Kuskokwim delta and Izembek Bay, Alaska; Humboldt Bay, California, and Scammons Lagoon, Baja California, Mexico. Smaller havens of safety on vital habitat areas will offer added survival insurance. Since the two first named areas in Alaska are already established as national wildlife ranges providing the nesting and nurturing grounds for the species, the current pressing need is to provide wintering habitats at Humboldt Bay, California, and Scammons Lagoon, Baja California. The accomplishment of these steps will offer the best conditions to perpetuate this fascinating maritime goose.

Black brant of the Pacific coast are not alone in showing sharp and startling variations in number. Brant geese all over the world are currently facing a common fate: attrition of safe habitat and sanctuary is causing a downward swing in population trends. Though this swing is more marked in some areas than in others, the pattern of decline is uniform.

In Europe, during the 1954 proceedings of the International Committee on Bird Preservation, held at Copenhagen between August 25 and September 3, several authors presented their views on the decline of the dark-breasted brant goose along those shores:

Lord Hurcomb, G.C.B., K.B.E. (United Kingdom), 1954, stated that the British Parliament recently passed a law affording complete protection throughout the year to the dark-breasted Brent Goose. He asked about its protection in Denmark. Professor Spärck informed him that it was only protected from January 1 to July 31, as is also the case in other countries (Germany).

Finn Salomonsen of the Zoological Museum of Copenhagen explained habitat changes and other menaces, referring particularly to gun pressure on the dwindling species:

The Dark-breasted Brent Goose, which breeds in Spitsbergen and on the continent from East Russia to Eastern Siberia, is threatened with extinction. In its high arctic breeding-places it is subject to extensive egg-collecting, and in many places, in its wintering grounds and along its migration routes it is heavily persecuted by hunters, although it is now protected in a number of countries. The main wintering ground extends from southern Scandinavia westward along the North Sea coasts to the British Isles. While the Pale-breasted Brent (*B. b. hrota*) is strictly protected in its American winter-quarter and the future existence of this form is assured, and while the population of the Pacific form (*B. b. nigricans*) amounts to about 175,000 individuals according to a recent census carried out by Leopold and Smith (California Fish and Game 39, 1953, p. 95-101), the decrease in the number of the Dark-breasted Brent wintering in N.W. Europe is alarming. The experienced ornithologists constituting the National Committees for Bird Preservation of the main wintering territories are unanimous that the total numbers of the Brent have seriously diminished and that the wintering population in N.W. Europe has probably now fallen below 20,000 individuals. The Brent has been badly hit not only by the still growing disturbances on its Arctic breeding-grounds, but still more severely by the widespread disappearance (since 1931) of its favourite food-plant, the Eel-Grass (*Zostera marina*), and by vast land-reclamation in its wintering grounds. In Denmark, where the Brent is not protected and where it, consequently, was heavily persecuted, a gradual decrease has taken place in the last 50 years. According to the Danish Game Statistics (started in 1940) the annual bag has dwindled from about 7000 in 1941 to 2500 in 1951. In Holland, where the Brent has been fully protected since 1949, more than 10,000 wintered before 1931 (when the Eel-Grass disappeared), but in recent years the number has decreased, and the wintering population does now (in 1953) not exceed 100 birds, while during spring migration (in April-May) the number may increase to about 300. Large land-reclamations are carried out in Holland at present, and if the so-called "Delta Plan" is carried out all tidal areas of the Wadden of the S.W. Netherlands will be closed from the sea and all Brents' haunts in this region vanish.

In a later paper (1958) Salomonsen described in detail the distribution and status of the brant population of the world; he also outlined his conclusion as to the causes of the general decline of these populations and offered remedial measures.

The brant family all over the world faces the same hazards. Whatever the area or climate, the two principal menaces to its survival are food shortage and man's thoughtlessness. Only constructive management, based on an enlightened attitude toward the balance of nature, can save this fascinating sea goose from extinction.

Bibliography

American Ornithologists Union
  1931 Check-list of North American birds, 4th ed., p. 419, Baltimore, Md.
  1957 Check-list of North American birds, 5th ed., Baltimore, Md.
Austin, O. L., and Nagahisa Kuroda
  1953 Birds of Japan, their status and distribution. Bull. Mus. Comp. Anat., Harvard.
Bailey, Florence Merriam
  1902 Handbook of birds of the western United States. Houghton Mifflin and Co., Boston and New York.
Baird, S. F., T. M. Brewer, and R. Ridgway
  1884 Water birds of North America. 1:473. Memoirs of the Museum of Comparative Zoology, Harvard University, Vol. 7.
Bent, Arthur Cleveland
  1925 Life histories of North American wildfowl. U.S. Nat. Mus. Bull. 130, U.S. National Museum, Washington, D.C., U.S. Govt. Printing Office, Washington, D.C.
Brandt, Herbert
  1943 Alaska bird trails, pp. 119-24, 272. Bird Research Foundation, Cleveland, Ohio.
Cade, Tom J.
  1953 Records of the black brant in the Yukon Basin and the question of a spring migration route. Journ. Wildl. Mgt., 19(2):321-24. Wildlife Society, Menasha, Wis.
Cottam, Clarence, John J. Lynch, and Arnold L. Nelson
  1944 Food habits and management of American sea brant. Journ. Wildl. Mgt., 8(1):36-56.
Dall, W. H., and H. M. Bannister
  1869 List of the birds of Alaska, with biographical notes. Transactions of the Chicago Acad. Sci., 1:267-325.

Delacour, Jean, and John T. Zimmer
  1952 Auk, January.
  1954 The waterfowl of the world, Vol. 1. Country Life Limited, London.
Denson, Eley P., Jr.
  1964 Comparison of waterfowl hunting techniques on Humboldt Bay, California. Journ. Wildl. Mgt., 28(1):103-20.
Dufresne, Frank
  1955 Little Black Goose. Field and Stream, 59:46-7, February.
Fay, Francis H.
  1960 The Pacific walrus. Alaska Sportsman, 26:14-15, November.
Gabrielson, Ira N., and Frederick C. Lincoln
  1959 The birds of Alaska, pp. 124-27. Stackpole Co., Harrisburg, Pa., and the Wildlife Management Institute, Washington, D.C.
Gabrielson, Ira N., and Stanley G. Jewett
  1940 Birds of Oregon. Oregon State Monographs, Oregon State System of Higher Education, Corvallis, Ore.
Gerow, James
  1944 Field note. Murrelet, 20:44. The State Museum, University of Washington, Seattle.
Gillham, C. E.
  1940 Unpublished field notes. U.S. Fish and Wildlife Service.
  1941 Unpublished field notes. U.S. Fish and Wildlife Service.
Handley, C. O., Jr.
  1950 The brant of Prince Patrick Island, Northwest Territories. Wilson Bull., 62:128-32.
Hansen, Henry A.
  1957 Utilization of wildlife by Alaska natives, p. 384. Unpublished report, U.S. Fish and Wildlife Service.
Hansen, Henry A. and Urban C. Nelson
  1957 Brant of the Bering Sea—migration and mortality, pp. 237-56. Transactions, 22nd North American Wildlife Conference, James B. Trefethen, ed. Wildlife Management Institute, Washington, D.C.
Hochbaum, Hans Albert
  1955 The travels and traditions of waterfowl. University of Minnesota Press, Minneapolis.
Hult, Ruby El
  1954 Untamed Olympics. Binfords and Mort, Portland, Ore.
Hunter, A.
  1889 Brant shooting at Smith's Island. Outing, 15:304, 360.
  1905 A close call, an episode of brant shooting. Outing, 45:4, January.
Jewett, S. G., W. P. Taylor, W. T. Shaw, and J. W. Aldrich
  1953 Birds of Washington State, pp. 106, 107, 108. University of Washington Press, Seattle.

Kortright, Francis H.
  1942 The ducks, geese and swans of North America. American Wildlife
        Institute, Washington, D.C.
Lauckhart, J. Burton
  1956 Calculating mortality rates for waterfowl. Murrelet, September-
        December.
Lawrence, George N.
  1848 Anser nigricans. Ann. Lyc. Nat. Hist., New York, 4:171, 172, pl.
        xii. Egg Harbor, N.J.
Leopold, A. Starker, and Robert H. Smith
  1953 Numbers and winter distribution of Pacific black brant in North
        America. Calif. Fish and Game, 39(1):95-101.
Lewis, Harrison
  1937 Migrations of the American brant. Auk, 54(1), January.
Mackay, R. H.
  1956 Black brant hunting in British Columbia, Winter, 1955-56 (mimeo.).
MacPhail, J. A.
  1891 Goose and brant on the Canadian coast. Outing, 17(6), March.
Mendall, Howard
  1958 The ringnecked duck in the northeast. University of Maine Bull.,
        60(16).
Moffitt, James
  1933 Brant notes. Calif. Fish and Game, 19(4).
  1937 Black brant population smaller, census reveals. Calif. Cons.,
        2(11):6.
  1937 Seventh annual black brant census in California. Calif. Fish and
        Game, 23(4):290-95.
  1938 Eighth annual black brant census in California. Calif. Fish and
        Game, 24(4).
  1939 Ninth annual black brant census in California. Calif. Fish and
        Game, 25(4):336.
  1941 Eleventh annual black brant census in California. Calif. Fish and
        Game, 27(4):216-33.
  1943 Twelfth annual black brant census in California. Calif. Fish and
        Game, 29(1):19-28.
Moffitt, James, and Clarence Cottam
  1941 Eelgrass depletion on the Pacific Coast and its effect on the black
        brant. U.S. Fish and Wildlife Service Leaflet 204, U.S. Dept. of
        Interior, Washington, D.C.
Munro, J. A.
  1957 Observations of winter waterfowl population at Morro Bay, Cali-
        fornia. Murrelet, 38(2), May-August.
Murie, Olaus J., and Victor B. Scheffer
  1959 Fauna of the Aleutian Islands and Alaska Peninsula. North Ameri-
        can Fauna, No. 61, U.S. Dept. of Interior.

Nelson, E. W.
    1886   Natural history of Alaska. U.S. Govt. Printing Office, Washington,
            D.C.
Nelson, Urban C.
    1952   Waterfowl banding and migrations in Alaska. Science in Alaska,
            pp. 201-7. Proceedings, 3rd Alaska Science Conference.
Osgood, W. H.
    1909   Biological investigations in Alaska and Yukon Territory. North
            American Fauna, No. 30.
Peters, James Lee
    1931   Check-list of birds of the world, 1:149-50. Harvard University
            Press, Cambridge, Mass.
Pleske, Theodore
    1928   Birds of the Eurasian tundra. Memoirs of the Boston Society of
            Natural History, 1(3).
Preble, E. A., and C. Hart Merriam
    1908   North American Fauna (27):307-9.
Price, W. W.
    1899   Some winter birds of the lower Colorado Valley. Condor, July 1,
            Stanford University.
Richardson, J.
    1851   Arctic searching expedition: A journal of a boat-voyage through
            Rupert's Land and the Arctic Sea, 2:111.
Salomonsen, Finn
    1954   Proceedings and papers of the fifth technical meeting, Interna-
            tional Committee on Bird Preservation. Copenhagen.
    1958   The present status of the brant goose (*Branta bernicla L.*) in west-
            ern Europe, pp. 43, 80. International Wildlife Research Bureau,
            No. 4.
Scott, Peter
    1951   Wild geese and Eskimos, pp. 145-49. Country Life Limited, Lon-
            don; Charles Scribner's Sons, New York.
Snyder, L. L.
    1957   Arctic birds of Canada. University of Toronto Press.
Spencer, Don L., U. C. Nelson, and W. A. Elkins
    1951   America's greatest goose-brant nesting area. Transactions, 16th
            North American Wildlife Conference, pp. 290-95.
Taverner, P. A.
    1928   Canada Dept. of Mines Bull. 41. Ottawa: F. A. Acland.
VanDyke, T. S.
    1891   Black brant at home. Outing, 19:222.
Williams, M. Y.
    1925   Notes on the life along the Yukon-Alaska boundary. Canadian
            Field-National, 39:69-72.

Natural science bulletins containing articles and references to the Pacific black brant include the following:

Condor, journal of the Cooper Ornithological Society, Department of Zoology, University of California at Los Angeles: July, 1905; September, 1911; March, 1920; May, 1921; March, 1922; September, 1925; November, 1933; March, 1941.

Murrelet, journal of northwestern mammalogy and ornithology, University of Puget Sound, Tacoma, Wash.: January, 1936; May-August, 1943; January-April, 1946.

Wilson Bulletin, quarterly magazine of ornithology, Wilson Ornithological Society, West Virginia University, Morgantown. December, 1927; September, 1930.

Index

abundance: reports on, 10-12, 126; fluctuations in, 18, 106, 109, 110; management regulation needs, 76; problems of limited species, 76-77; decline in, 106-8, 126; predictions of, 96, 108; analysis of, 109-12; problems in measuring, 111; significance of, 112

Adair, John: reporting on Alaska migration, 55; jaegers, 63

adaptability: limited, 124-25

adult birds: described, 7; calls, 26; diet, 30; hunted, 48, 77; migration south, 52; effect of molting, 63

aerial ability: maneuvers in mating, 35-36, 37; in survival, 63

age-class survival differential: importance of, 97-98

air flights: in Alaska, 61-62; aid to hunters, 85

air investigation: problems of, 29, 67, 109-10

airplanes: reaction to, 67

Alaska: distribution of brant, 9, 10-11; game commission, 11; seasonal range, 9-12; Gulf of, 12, 50; migration from, 12, 50-53, 56; importance of diet in, 30; activity of mated birds, 38; nesting activity, 40, 44; nonbreeding birds, 50; migration to, 54-55; sled dogs, 60-62; predators, 59-68; hazards to survival in, 69-70; human molestation, 70; hunting areas, 77-86; Eskimo hunters, 77-86; refuges, range of, 81, 120, 121-23; waterfowl distribution, 84; effect of statehood on management practices, 85, 122; tourism a factor in hunting, 85; air transportation a factor in hunting, 85-86; harvest in, 91; Eskimo practices, 113-16; refuges established, 122, 125; research in, 124

Alaskan Arctic: migration routes, 10-11; mating, 38-40; nesting, 40-42, 54

Alaskan Peninsula: migration, 12, 50; nesting season, 38, 40; refuge, 121

Aleutian Islands: occurrence of brant, 12; hunting, 77

American Ornithologists Union Check-list: on distribution, 4, 9, 10, 16, 19

annual orbit. See migration

arctic: nesting in, 9, 10, 16, 36; migration patterns, 9-12, 49, 54; range of brant, 10; effect of weather on nesting, 42; goslings, 47; predators, 59-67; Eskimos, 79; waterfowl management, 113-16. See also Alaskan Arctic; Canadian